I0643910

on track ...

The Chic Organisation

every album, every song

Chris Sutton

SONICBOND

sonicbondpublishing.com

Sonicbond Publishing Limited
www.sonicbondpublishing.co.uk
Email: info@sonicbondpublishing.co.uk

First Published in the United Kingdom 2025
First Published in the United States 2025

British Library Cataloguing in Publication Data:
A Catalogue record for this book is available from the British Library

ISBN 978-1-78952-366-9

Typeset in ITC Garamond Std & ITC Avant Garde Gothic
Printed and bound in England

Graphic design and typesetting: Full Moon Media

Follow us on social media:
Twitter: https://twitter.com/SonicbondP
Instagram: www.instagram.com/sonicbondpublishing_/
Facebook: www.facebook.com/SonicbondPublishing/

Linktree QR code:

Dedication

Dedicated to Anne Ellis and Julia Lowndes with much love and thanks for their constant support and friendship.

Would you like to write for Sonicbond Publishing?

We are mainly a music publisher, but we also occasionally publish in other genres including film and television. At Sonicbond Publishing we are always on the look-out for authors, particularly for our two main series, On Track and Decades.

Mixing fact with in depth analysis, the On Track series examines the entire recorded work of a particular musical artist or group. All genres are considered from easy listening and jazz to 60s soul to 90s pop, via rock and metal.

The Decades series singles out a particular decade in an artist or group's history and focuses on that decade in more detail than may be allowed in the On Track series.

While professional writing experience would, of course, be an advantage, the most important qualification is to have real enthusiasm and knowledge of your subject. First-time authors are welcomed, but the ability to write well in English is essential.

Sonicbond Publishing has distribution throughout Europe and North America, and all our books are also published in E-book form. Authors will be paid a royalty based on sales of their book. Further details about our books are available from www.sonicbondpublishing.com. To contact us, complete the contact form there or email info@sonicbondpublishing.co.uk

on track ...

The Chic Organisation

Contents

Interviews and notes

My thanks to the following for their participation in this book: Alva Chinn, Eddie Daniels, Sammy Figueroa, Jean Fineberg, Stan Harrison, Bill Holloman, Kenny Lehman, Ellen Seeling, Roger Squitero, Jessica Wagner and Tony Wright.

The Chic Organisation personnel are prioritised in the album credits (apart from the principal artists in the case of their work with external clients). This is intended to aid reference and in no way downplays the contributions of the 'non-Chic' musicians.

The best mixes/masters of the albums were created by Steven Wilson and released to streaming services in 2023. His work has brought a new clarity to the albums without losing the original production design. So far, the first five Chic albums and Sister Sledge's *We Are Family* are available. It is hoped that a physical release of these Hi-Res mixes in stereo and 5.1 surround sound will one day be made available.

Many remixes have been created as these albums have been slowly reissued. Principal among them are those by Dimitri From Paris. For an easy way to get all of his Chic Organisation remixes, readers should check out his Bandcamp page, where his album *Dimitri From Paris Presents Le Chic Remix* is available. His work is an essential listen as he presents the songs in intriguing new mixes, often featuring elements which didn't make the original final mix. He has also created instrumental mixes of all the songs he worked on.

While this book focuses on the songs, there are two books which are more biographical in nature. Nile Rodgers' autobiography *Le Freak* and Daryl Easlea's *Chic And The Politics Of Disco* are both excellent further reading and are referenced on occasion here. There is one superb CD box set compilation – *The Chic Organisation Box Set Volume 1: Savoir Faire.* This is abbreviated to *Savoir Faire* in the comments.

Who Were The Chic Organisation?

The Chic Organisation was an umbrella term used for the collective of musicians appearing on the records discussed in this book. At the heart of it was the actual Chic Organisation partnership, which was solely between Nile Rodgers and Bernard Edwards. The other musicians and singers involved were paid wages for their services, but three were also used for promotional purposes. In *Le Freak,* Rodgers talked about drummer Tony Thompson being 'formally hired' to 'role-play' for press and publicity photos. As time went on, it would rankle with Thompson that he was not part of the Rodgers and Edwards partnership. Equally part of the promotional side were singers Alfa Anderson and Luci Martin. Because Thompson, Anderson and Martin were involved in the promotional aspects, it made Chic look essentially like a five-person group, understandably leading to assumptions that they were equal group members with Rodgers and Edwards.

Key Personnel From The 'Classic' Era Of The Chic Organisation (1977 – 1984)

Alfa Anderson

She first appears on the debut album as part of the Chic Choir. Following the first tour, she was lead and harmony vocalist from the C'est Chic album onwards, also appearing on the Organisation's work for other clients. She was a key member for publicity photos and appearances.

The Chic Brass

Jean Fineberg (saxophone) and Ellen Seeling (trumpet) were recruited for the first Chic tour and also recorded brass parts for C'est Chic, We Are Family, Risqué and the near title track of Love Somebody Today.

The Chic Strings

There were several members, including pre-eminent members Marianne Carroll, Valerie Haywood, Cheryl Hong and Karen Milne. Others include Claire Bergman and Karen Karlsrud. The strings first appeared on C'est Chic and remained a vital part of most albums and live shows.

Michelle Cobbs

She joined for touring purposes initially, and then sang on Risqué, along with Fonzi Thornton. She then contributed to most of the albums as harmony/backing vocalist.

Bernard Edwards

Co-founder of the Chic Organisation, he was the co-producer, writer, arranger and bass player on the classic era albums. He was also a member of the pre-Chic band New York City. Edwards' bass playing was a significant part of the Chic sound.

Sammy Figueroa

The legendary percussionist appeared on the debut album and then recorded on the majority of the albums in this era.

Ray Jones

The piano and keyboards player joined the Organisation when he was 19 and played on many of the records from C'est Chic onwards. He also toured with Chic.

Kenny Lehman

A woodwind player, songwriter and producer, he was a key part of the setup for the debut album. He parted ways with Rodgers and Edwards after the recording of Chic and Norma Jean Wright's album.

Luci Martin
The lead and harmony vocalist first came in for the tour supporting the debut album. She was also part of the publicity for the band as one of 'the five faces' of Chic.

Nile Rodgers
The guitarist/vocalist/songwriter/producer was co-owner of the Organisation. His guitar style has often been imitated and his influence has been felt across the musical spectrum. He continues to lead Nile Rodgers & Chic and often guest appears with other artists.

Rob Sabino
The keyboard and synth wizard started with Rodgers and Edwards in New York City and stayed with them working on most of the Organisation albums, as well as some touring duties.

Andy Schwartz
He was recruited on piano/keyboards for the debut album and contributed to many of the other records, as well as being touring member.

Tony Thompson
Chic's powerhouse drummer was there from the New York City days. He appears on all of the records in the classic era and was one of the five in the publicity photos.

Fonzi Thornton
The harmony and lead vocalist joined Chic in time for Risqué and subsequent touring. He was with them on most of the Organisation's records and still works with Nile Rodgers & Chic on occasions.

Norma Jean Wright
She was the original lead vocalist, brought in for the debut album. Her own album was also recorded with the Organisation. She did part of the first tour and was featured in publicity photos and appearances.

In The Beginning – The Big Apple Band

Nile Rodgers (born 19 September 1952 in New York City) studied guitar at the Manhattan School of Music. His early bands included the jazz/rock fusion New World Rising and a touring version of the *Sesame Street* TV show. Bernard Edwards (born 31 October 1952 in Greenville, North Carolina) started his musical career on saxophone and then guitar, swapping over to bass while a teenager. In 1973, Edwards became the musical director for r&b vocal band New York City, best remembered for their smash hit 'I'm Doing Fine Now'. His key duty was to assemble a backing band for the singers, which he called the Big Apple Band. Rodgers, by now a firm friend of Edwards, came in on guitar, while Rob Sabino came in on keyboards. The original drummer was only named as 'Clyde' by Rodgers in *Le Freak*. He left and was replaced for a short time by Woody Cunningham. The Big Apple Band didn't play on any of New York City's records, but the run of live dates gave them the experience of playing in front of big audiences.

They also started to play dates in their own right, securing the services of Robert Cotter on vocals. They had seen him sing with his band, Best Of Both Worlds, who had been the house band in a touring production of *Jesus Christ Superstar* (*JCS*). More significantly than Cotter's recruitment, the band acquired a new drummer, Tony Thompson. He was, in fact, their second choice; their first choice had been the too-young (at 15) Omar Hakim. He would return to the Chic orbit in 1982.

The Big Apple Band setlist featured songs written by Rodgers and Edwards, plus some by Sabino, as well as disco and r&b covers. The band were tight and good enough that it felt worthwhile to record some demos, which were produced by Leon Pendarvis (the *Saturday Night Live* band producer). Rodgers told Ian Meldrum on the Australian TV show *Countdown* in 1979: 'Now when we hear them, they sound pretty decent for a young band. But when the tapes got out there, it was pretty different. All of the companies that we gave our tapes to kept the songs and said, 'Wow, the group are great, now let's see a picture of them', and it was five black guys and one white guy!' At best, record companies were confused by the look of the band!

For the curious, Rodgers explained in the *Very Best Of Chic* CD notes (2000) how the band's sound worked: 'I'd take these jazz standards and do disco arrangements of them, like *Porgy And Bess*. The record the band made never came out, but that's how we got involved with the concept of dance music.' That record he mentions is tantalising; presumably, he still has the unreleased tracks tucked away.

Nothing else was known about The Big Apple Band's music until, surprisingly, Rodgers put two black-and-white promo videos of them up on YouTube. Kenny Lehman (who was Robert Cotter's flatmate) confirms that it was he who recorded the footage of what is a lively, vibrant band running through two energetic cover versions. This performance likely dates from between October and December 1976. The lineup is Robert Cotter (vocals), Nile Rodgers (guitar, vocals), Bernard Edwards (bass, vocals), Tony Thompson (drums) and Rob Sabino (keyboards).

First up is the Bee Gees' 'You Should Be Dancing'. They released it in June 1976 on their *Children Of The World* album. By September, it had also been a number-one hit single in the US and reached number five in the UK. The Big Apple Band version is a pretty straight cover version but without the brass they might have added if it had been covered in the Chic years. Rodgers gets a short, flashy solo, but that's the only real difference to the Bee Gees version in this solid, energetic piece of work.

'Getaway' follows. Earth, Wind And Fire released this in 1976 as a single and it charted at number 12 in the US. It was taken from their album *Spirit,* released on 28 September 1976. The jazzy tones of this excellent song suit the embryonic Chic down to the ground. Cotter is still very much the odd man out. He doesn't sound 'right', but that is partly because we know there is better to come without him in the future. There is a real burn and intensity to the music, a harder energy to it than Chic would deploy until it started to appear in their music in the 1980s. It's a compelling song that ends suddenly and leaves you wanting more.

Missing You (Robert Cotter) (1976)

Personnel:
Robert Cotter: lead vocals
Nile Rodgers: guitar, backing vocals
Bernard Edwards: bass
Tony Thompson: drums, percussion
Rob Sabino: keyboards, Fender Rhodes
Kenny Lehman: saxophone, flute (whole album)
Produced by Robert Cotter and Lee Grayson in New York, 1976
Release date: 1976, 2021 (reissue)
Label: Tiger Lily/Wewantsounds
Highest chart places: UK: did not chart, US: did not chart
Running time: 38:33

Robert Cotter got a deal with Tiger Lily Records for a solo album, which featured the nascent Chic. Recording dates are unknown, but it seems feasible that it was put together around the end of 1976, sometime around or after when those two live tracks were recorded. The credits listed above are just for the two tracks the Big Apple Band appear on. While the other tracks have their moments, it's these two that are of major concern for Chic completists. Sadly for Cotter, his fortune was short-lived; the album initially vanished without a trace due, allegedly, to the label being a tax scam venture of owner Morris Levy. It has since seen a limited re-release on CD.

'Love Rite' (Cotter)
Many of the Chic components are present and correct here. Edwards and Rodgers have the groove in place and Thompson's cymbals have a sizzle that would come to be a trademark. Sabino's Fender Rhodes has a warm, jazzy feel, more indistinct than his later work with Chic. Rodgers gets a solo, which is good without being astonishing, but it works for the song. Cotter's falsetto vocals are good enough, but in the final analysis, this is an average piece of work that would attract little interest but for the Chic connections. That being said, the instrumental track would have worked a treat as part of a film or TV score.

'Saturday' (Cotter/Rodgers/Edwards)
This sounds almost like a demo for the more sumptuous later version with Norma Jean. Rodgers' guitar work is sketchier and less full, with Sabino carrying the melody alone on keyboards. It feels so much sparser without the strings, etc. Cotter sings alone, too, and while he is adequate on the verses, he misses the lift on the choruses with the Chic singers. Somebody (possibly Rodgers) *does* sing along with him, but it's not as impressive. The best part is the middle eight ('if you left it up to me every day would Saturday'), which has a taut, minimal force to it that is more diluted on the Norma Jean version. This one is worth hearing, but the Norma Jean version is still better.

Cotter was fired from the Big Apple Band (for reasons unknown), and for a time, the band continued as a four-piece. A name change was then forced on them when a different Big Apple Band emerged. This incarnation (led by Walter Murphy) had a hit track on the *Saturday Night Fever* soundtrack called 'A Fifth Of Beethoven'. It was Edwards who initially came up with the name Chic, which they felt summed up their attitude and musical direction. Rodgers recalled in the *Very Best Of Chic* CD notes in 2000: 'That's when the whole concept of disco became so exciting to us. I thought, 'Wow, I can use my jazz chops and my harmonic knowledge and still write a good pop melody over it.' Those same notes reported Edwards' assessment of the new band: 'Chic is about good vibes, good grooves and good clothes. That's all we talked about – the fantasy life.' Now, all they had to do was work up some material and get a record deal!

Chic's Studio Methods And Style

Although it didn't happen instantaneously Chic evolved as an r&b band with influences ranging from jazz, funk, rock and, yes, even disco! Rodgers and Edwards' songwriting partnership was driven by Rodgers, as most of the songs' initial sketches came from him. Edwards would then add his ideas and the songs would come together. It sometimes worked the other way around, but this was not usual.

The duo were also the core of the music. Arguably, the most recognisable facet of the Chic sound is Rodgers' rhythm guitar. His guitar of choice has long been the 'Hitmaker', a 1960 Fender Stratocaster with a '59 neck. He spoke to Amit Sharma for *Guitar World* in October 2020 about how he settled on it as his go-to guitar:

> I was basically a jazz and classical player, to begin with. The speed I could achieve using my fingers, I couldn't achieve with a pick. I found it easier with my hands. Bernard was a really funk-oriented guy, and he hated my sound with the big, fat, jazzy guitar (a Gibson Barney Kessel). He'd say it fed back too much, and, therefore, you couldn't play it loud, etc. There was an opening act on our tour and I let their guitarist use my equipment. He was playing a Stratocaster and was really chugging on it. That's when I realised what Bernard was trying to get me to do. He talked me into buying a Strat, so I did. And that was the Hitmaker, bought in 1973 from a little pawn shop in Florida.

As for effects pedals, Rodgers admitted: 'I'm quite simple; my pedalboard only has three things on it – a chorus, a wah and maybe an overdrive, which I don't really use.' Rodgers' tone was, and still is, usually clean and bright with a focus on the high and high-mid tones.

Bernard Edwards's formidable bass playing, although not always as instantly recognisable, was almost as key to the Chic sound as Rodgers' guitar. For the first Chic album, he used a Precision bass, swapping over to a 1977 Music Man Stingray (with round wound strings) for every album after that. Rodgers explained his partner's unusual technique to *Bass Player* in November 2023:

> Bernard was a guitar player before he played the bass guitar. But the last thing he wanted to be was a bass player who used a pick. So he played with his forefinger and thumb as if he were holding a pick. He'd strike the string with the bottom and top of his finger. The strength of the low-end comes from his thumb on top and the other three fingers curled up underneath, so he had the fattest pick you could ever imagine!

The third man in the expanded rhythm department was their powerhouse drummer. Tony Thompson had to adapt quickly to the wishes of Rodgers and Edwards, moreso the former. He explained to *Modern Drummer* in 2002:

> When I first joined, Nile was like: 'Why do you need all those cymbals and stuff?' He would tell Bernard, 'The brother plays way too much.' So Bernard took me under his wing. He told me: 'Get rid of all that shit. Just keep a bass drum, snare and hi-hat. When you master that, then maybe I'll add another cymbal or drum.' So, I was spoon-fed my kit. But it worked. It's amazing how creative you get from boredom. You come up with all these different things. Nile and Bernard saw a lot of things in me that I didn't see in myself. They helped me immensely in learning to groove.

Also contributing backing tracks were Rob Sabino (keyboards) and Sammy Figueroa (percussion).

The band moved fast when recording. It's known, for instance, that the backing tracks on *C'est Chic* and *We Are Family* were all done within the same two weeks. Percussionist Sammy Figueroa recalls: 'We all played together like we were playing a concert. The studio was completely open and a lot of those songs were done in one take.' Rodgers expanded on this to *Sound On Sound* in April 2005: 'The rhythm track was always played completely live, without a click track, and we'd select one particular take. No song that we ever recorded was compiled from different takes. We knew which take it was because that's the one we kept.' Once the 'best' rhythm track, which also included Rodgers' rhythm guitar and often keyboards, was selected, they would swiftly move on to overdubs and vocals. It was common for them to record all the strings and brass in two or three days, with any other instrumental overdubs and all of the vocals taking about the same length of time.

As as writing the material and playing on it, Rodgers and Edwards also produced the records, sometimes with assistance. A key man in the studio on most of the early Chic Organisation records was the legendary Bob Clearmountain, who has worked on many massive hit albums.
Crispin Cioe caught up with him for *High Fidelity* in September 1979. He explained how they got the sounds down:

> With Chic, I go for a live sound that is recorded very cleanly. Bernard and Nile will rarely use all 24 tracks on their tunes, and we try to do as much live playing as possible. I close-mic the instruments, with 12 to 16 mics on the drums alone, so we get virtually no leakage. We also get a tight sound in the small room and they're playing live, with each other.

The Chic Organisation also wrote, played on and produced many records for other artists. Rodgers explained their philosophy on these projects to *Freeze Frame* in 1981: 'We have a certain formula for doing what we do. However, we absolutely write and produce differently for each one of those artists. We have to understand these people's artistry and try to develop that with our interpretation of them.' Once they had settled on the songs and recorded the backing tracks, they would bring in the artists to sing. Rodgers commented to *Sound On Sound* in April 2005:

> We never did guide vocals, and no vocalists ever heard the song before they recorded any of our records, even if they were stars. Hearing these records for the first time, the artists were excited by them and wanted to prove they could do a good job. That made them concentrate and give a fresh, exciting performance. At the same time, the way Bernard and I worked with vocalists, we'd really coach and push them. We had a very definite idea as to what kind of vocal we needed.

Rodgers is 'forgetting' there that Fonzi Thornton (regular backing/harmony singer) recorded guide vocals for Diana Ross and Johnny Mathis at least. There were some stars you clearly didn't spring a vocal on, but Sister Sledge and Norma Jean Wright were among those who *did* record vocals with no prior knowledge of the song.

The final track selection and sequencing had a formula, as Rodgers partly explained to *Sound On Sound* in April 2005:

> The concept of a Chic album is that we're the opening act for a really big star, and we're unknown. No-one has ever heard of us; we're brand new and we're a live band coming out on stage to tell everybody who we are. So, there's always a song on the album that announces we're Chic – on the first album, it's 'Strike Up The Band'; on the second, it's 'Chic Cheer', and so on. The concept is that we're an r&b band playing live for an old-time r&b audience. They came to see the star, but the opening act was important, too, so the opening act had to put on a really good show.

As well as the albums, a key facet of their success was the huge hit singles – a sparkling array of gems recorded under their own name and for other artists. A facet they had in common was opening with the chorus. It set the songs up immediately, straight into the hook, and made for an interesting dynamic of shifting to the verse rather than vice versa. Another key feature, more often used in the album tracks, was the 'breakdown', where the song was stripped down to the basics and built back up again. These are some of the finest passages in Chic's output.

If there was a weakness to the songs, then it was definitely the lyrics. But the feel and emotion in the vocals were usually more than enough to compensate.

The groove and feel of their songs often saw them categorised as a disco band. Initially, they had embraced it because – as Rodgers told James Truman of *Melody Maker* in 1979 – 'Disco gave us the perfect opportunity to realise our concept because it wasn't about being black, white, male or female. Furthermore, it would give us a chance to get into the mainstream.' Edwards had been less keen, admitting to Truman: 'I realised if we did it our way, it'd be pretty good.'

The links to disco didn't take long, two years at most, to prove a problem. The sometimes derogatory press inferences about their quality and musical credibility rightly infuriated them. Edwards indignantly made it clear to Danny Baker in *New Musical Express* in January 1979 that the band had musical chops: 'The two of us, with our drummer Tony Thompson, could walk into a studio and sweat off some stuff that could floor these so-called serious music guys.' But the band, in essence, were all about the groove. Within that, there was still room for dazzling musical passages and solos. There was more going on in the likes of 'Good Times' or 'I Want Your Love' than much of the material in the disco genre that hit the charts.

Baker, having seen them on *Top Of The Pops* (*TOTP*), wondered how much of the style was planned out. 'Oh, I wouldn't say planned at all', replied Edwards. He continued:

> I always thought that presenting an all-male show, like The Commodores, is really lacking something. So the girls (Anderson and Martin) are looking great, singing great and it all helps tone down the black funky impression that a lot of bands put over. The three women who play violins are very important, too, for our balance, our look and our sound. Even though I dislike a lot of strings on a disc, I think they add a necessary sweetener to our rhythm.

Chic (Chic) (1977)

Personnel:
Nile Rodgers: guitar, backing vocals
Bernard Edwards: bass, lead vocals on 'You Can Get By'
Tony Thompson: drums, percussion (except 'Dance, Dance, Dance')
Norma Jean Wright: lead vocals on 'Everybody Dance', 'Est-Ce Que C'est Chic?' and 'Falling In Love With You', backing vocals
Rob Sabino, Andy Schwartz: keyboards, piano
Alfa Anderson, Robin Clark, Diva Gray, David Lasley, Luther Vandross: harmony and backing vocals
David Friedman: vibraphone on 'Everybody Dance' and 'You Can Get By'
Tom Coppola: keyboards, clavinet on 'Everybody Dance' and 'Strike Up The Band'
Sammy Figueroa, Gerardo Velez: percussion
Eddie Martinez: guitar overdubs on 'Everybody Dance'
Jimmy Young: drums on 'Dance, Dance, Dance'
George Young: flute, tenor saxophone
Vito Rendace: flute, tenor saxophone on 'Dance, Dance, Dance'
Jay Beckenstein: saxophone solo on 'Sao Paolo'
Barry Rogers: trombone
Jon Faddis: trumpet
Gloria Agostini: harp
Kenny Lehman: woodwind arrangements
Alfred Brown: strings
Produced and arranged by Bernard Edwards, Kenny Lehman and Nile Rodgers at Electric Lady Studios and Power Station (New York), 1977
'Everybody Dance' original tracks produced and engineered at Sound Ideas (New York) by Robert Drake, 1977
Release date: 22 November 1977
Label: Atlantic
Highest chart places: UK: did not chart, US: 27
Running time: 38:33
All songs by Edwards and Rodgers, except as noted.

The first song to be recorded was 'Everybody Dance'. Their friend Robert Drake was an engineer and de facto producer at the Sound Ideas studio, and he let them in to record the song out of hours during the studio's downtime. A test pressing of the song proved a success, wowing the customers of the Night Owl Club in New York, where Drake worked as a DJ.

Things started to move when Edwards got a gig playing bass on a song called 'I Love New York' (a huge song by Steve Karmen), which was being produced/arranged by Kenny Lehman. Lehman had been looking for a B-side for the song and was interested in using Rodgers and Edwards for it, but he went with an instrumental take of the A-side instead when he realised just how promising a proposition the duo were, feeling instead that their destiny lay beyond a throw away track. Lehman recalls:

> At that point in time, I had these two investors, Marc Kreiner and Tom Cossie, with whom I was partnered in Turtle Productions. They wanted to get into the music business, so they hired me as their partner. I said to Marc and Tom, 'I have two guys I think I can write and work with; we have a good shot at creating something because these guys are really talented.' They said they were willing to take the risk and gave me $12,000. I went to Nile and Bernard and said, 'Look, let's write something together. Let's do an A-side and a B-side.'

Rodgers recalled in *Le Freak* that Lehman came to him with a jam track recorded by Edwards and a session drummer named Jimmy Young. Lehman, said Rodgers, asked him if he had anything to go with it. What Rodgers had was the hook of 'Dance, Dance, Dance', which Edwards simplified. Lehman continues:

> We went to Electric Lady, and the three of us wrote and produced two songs. I did all the strings and the horns and featured myself on sax on 'Sao Paolo'. We didn't have a band yet, so we used studio players. We didn't use Tony Thompson on 'Dance, Dance, Dance'. I wanted to keep Jimmy Young, who had a much stronger backbeat. Tony was going to be used for the album, but we wanted it stronger and simpler for this song.

Thompson (who is on 'Sao Paolo') recalled to *Modern Drummer* (2002) that 'We pressed 'Dance, Dance, Dance' without a record deal. Back then, you could go over to a hot club, ask the DJ to play it and see the results, which is what we did. And people just freaked. From there, we signed to Atlantic.' That's an oversimplification because the song was picked up first by Buddah Records, as Lehman explains:

> I went to all these labels, including Atlantic, and they all turned me down. A friend of mine, Roger Bell, said I should go to a record plugger named Bud Holland and tell him that if he sold 'Dance, Dance Dance' to a label, my partners and I would give him the money he needed to finish his album. So, I told Bud this, and he said, 'Let me hear it.' So, I played it for him and he said, 'I can sell this.' Sure enough, it got accepted, and 'Dance, Dance, Dance' came out on Buddah Records.

Buddah released it as a promo single, backed with 'Sao Paolo'. It was executive produced by Kreiner, who, along with Cossie, then brokered a deal with Atlantic. Their president, Jerry Greenberg, was hugely enthusiastic about the song. He recounted to *Freeze Frame* in 1981 how he came to sign Chic:

> Tom Cossie told me that he had just entered into a production deal and picked up 'Dance, Dance, Dance' by a group called Chic. He came over and played me the record and I loved it. We had some other people come down and hear the record and they all got very excited, and it was like a signing in minutes. I had never met the guys; it was just from hearing the sound of their first record.

The final plot twist saw an indignant Buddah taking up the situation with Atlantic, who (to avoid legal action) allowed Buddah to release their single as well! Time now to record their debut album. The recording budget was $35,000, and it was recorded in under three weeks.

Four songs had been demoed at Sound Ideas, with Rob Drake engineering: 'Everybody Dance', 'Strike Up The Band', 'Sao Paolo' and 'Est-Ce Que C'est Chic'. With 'Dance, Dance, Dance' since recorded, it only left them to find three more songs. Also recorded was a cover version of 'Bess, You Is My Woman Now' (a Big Apple Band holdover) from the musical *Porgy And Bess*. Much more work was definitely done on 'Everybody Dance', with vocal verses added to the demo recording to finish it off.

Luther Vandross came in to sing on the album and he brought in David Lasley, Robin Clark and Alfa Anderson. Vandross first came across Rodgers when he was brought in by arranger Paul Riser to play on the *This Close To You* album, recorded in 1976 by his band Luther. Rodgers was grateful for the opportunity, which he credited in *Le Freak* as his big break into the 'studio scene'. Lasley came in *after* 'Dance, Dance, Dance' and he said that all the vocals were done in two days at Power Station. Diva Gray (aka Deborah Gray) was also brought in on vocals at the suggestion of Lehman.

Lehman points out: 'We brought in the best musicians. I did all the arranging, orchestrating and producing with Nile and Bernard. I hired the brass section and I also played on things as a soloist.' Lehman also sorted out the strings: 'What I did was I had a concertmaster and a first violinist, and then I had Alfred (Brown) contract the rest of the strings.'

One keyboard player who is often thought to have taken part was Spyro Gyra's Jeremy Wall. He says: 'Nope, I was with Spyro Gyra then. I never played on the Chic record.' But there were still *three* keyboard players credited apart from Wall. Lehman said, 'I would have said Rob Sabino did the whole album', and that seems very likely, with Tom Coppola and Andy Schwartz chipping in.

To augment Thompson, they used two percussionists. The now legendary Sammy Figueroa was the primary percussionist. He recalled:

> The Chic records came years after I had played with so many other people. Nile called me out of the blue and he said, 'Look, we are at Power Station doing our first record and we would love you to play on it. Tell me how much you need.' He told me, 'We start at ten and we finish at ten at night

> and we are going to be in there for four days.' So, I found out what the hours cost and I said, 'Look, I can do it for four days; I'll bring the percussion, but you have to rent the heavy stuff.' He said, 'Fine.' I told him what I wanted and he said, 'Yes.' I didn't have to carry a lot with me – a bag with all my shakers, wood blocks and cowbells and all kinds of whistles. I went to the studio and we worked for four days non-stop. I was on just about the whole album because I was the main percussionist. Geraldo Velez was a guest player who came in for one tune.

As well as the already formidable lineup of vocalists they had coming in, Norma Jean Wright was recruited to sing the female lead vocals. She recalled to David Nathan of *Classic Soul* in November 1978: 'Just to kind of assure themselves that I was the right person for the role of lead singer, Nile and Bernard came down to check me out at Broady's, a night spot in New York, and that kinda sealed it all.'

Oddly, she only sang lead on the first three tracks on side two, and it turned out to be her first and last album under the Chic name. When she was laying down the vocals for 'Falling In Love With You', Cossie and Kreiner suggested that she should record her own album. Wright admitted to Nathan: 'Bernard and Nile and I had already talked about it from the beginning, but I didn't think we'd get to it quite so soon. I figured it would happen maybe a year or so after being with Chic, but everyone felt that it should be the next recording project when the Chic album was completed.'

The album's packaging is a let-down. The front cover shows an uncredited Valentine Monnier and Alva Chinn. Photographer Frank Laffitte captured a playful moment with the two, whistles at the ready, looking as though they are in a discotheque. The warm, saturated colour tones heighten the impression of heat. Chinn recalls:

> For me, it was just a shoot. At the time, I didn't have Halston, Chloe or anything as work. I was just booked for this little job and I don't even know who chose us. I didn't even know the photographer. We didn't have much interaction between the two of us (her and Monnier). I didn't even know her, to be honest with you; when it's somebody I know, it's much easier to have fun. I don't even remember them playing music while we posed.

As for the whistles and the gauzy, sweaty look, she said: 'I would like it to have been more than the two of us with whistles. The final look was done that way to make it look like we were in a hot, steamy club. We were just sitting there, not even standing. If he had pulled the camera out, it would have looked real boring. But isn't it great that a photograph can give you a whole story that wasn't actually happening?' Chinn went on to be one of the world's top models. 'I did mostly fashion work and magazines, but I still get people saying, 'Oh, you were on the Chic cover!"

The problem with the cover is two-fold. Firstly, there's no Chic presence on it, and secondly, it just doesn't relate to the sophistication and style of the music. The back cover is even worse: a stark list of credits on a white background. Fortunately, the cheap, forgettable packaging didn't seem to affect sales in America, which saw the album go top 30.

Putting sales aside, what we have here is a band working out what they are about. Even at this early stage, behind the glamour and silky smooth grooves, there were already subtexts to be heard in the lyrics. For example, the fatiguing dance marathons on 'Dance, Dance, Dance'. 'We'd always have to stick in the deep, hidden meaning', said Rodgers on the *Very Best Of Chic* notes in 2000. Sometimes, the album hits home, but there are one or two misses/diversions that don't work so well. Lehman remains proud of it, though: 'I think there's a lot of great stuff on the album. Maybe my involvement is why it sounds jazzier than the later albums.' Rodgers also saw a lot of merit. He told David Nathan of *Classic Soul* in July 1979: 'For me, artistic fulfilment came when we did tracks like 'Savoir Faire' and 'Sao Paolo' because it allowed me to stretch out and do something different.' As for his rhythm playing, Lehman commented: 'Nile's style of rhythm guitar was different; it was a risk because nobody else was playing like that. But ultimately, as he developed with Bernard, it became influential. It changed the whole disco sound.'

The best track (Lehmann agrees too) is 'Everybody Dance'. Looking ahead, Rodgers and Edwards would assume control of the records. Without having to collaborate, their focus would be much sharper. As Figueroa pointed out, 'Before you knew it, they had won a Grammy and it never stopped – the hit records continued. They were just on top of the world.'

'Dance, Dance, Dance (Yowsah, Yowsah, Yowsah)' (Edwards/Kenny Lehman/Rodgers)

Rodgers and Edwards wanted a strong vocal hook for the song. Rodgers told *The Daily News* in 1977: 'We finally thought of how Gig Young kept saying 'Yowsah, yowsah, yowsah' in *They Shoot Horses, Don't They?*' The 1969 film focused on the dance marathon contests of 1930s America. Kenny Lehman came up with the orchestral sweetening and also provided the nasal 'megaphone' voice-over with the aid of a filter cutting out the low and high frequencies.

It must be the most understated intro of any of the Chic 'big hitter' songs, coming in on Edwards' bass pulse, the cymbals and then Rodgers' guitar. Some of the fatigue of those dance contests feels almost present in the quite dense bottom end, although it has a delicious groove to it. The string arrangement lacks the variation and melodic flair that comes on the later records, but it works well enough as a higher melodic texture.

The lead vocals are shared by Vandross, Gray and Clark and they have an 'anonymity' to them that means they blend into the music. Lehman confirmed that 'Vandross is singing in the chorus, and I think you can also hear him in the verses.' Of the instrumentalists, big plaudits go to Figueroa, or Velez, for the percussion touches that pepper the track, such as, for example, at 0:46 for the 'Rhumba and Tango' line, etc.

The breakdown at 2:05 reduces down to Vandross intoning the title, drums and handclaps. The next build-up isn't one of their best, apart from the cinematic strings and brass section (including Kenny Lehman on woodwind) that come in. At the four-minute mark, you would expect it to fade out, but instead, they keep it going by way of Sabino with a wonderful jazzy synth solo. Things really pick up with it. Rodgers gets to solo after that, playing around the melody. He doesn't stretch far from it, but it makes for an enthralling section as he, Edwards and Thompson are the focal point, locked in together.

As a statement of intent, it was perfect, with enough about it to warrant its status as a classic, despite being at least two minutes too long. The single was released in October 1977, reaching number six in America. It was released in Britain in November 1977 and also got to number six.

'São Paolo' (Edwards/Kenny Lehman/Rodgers)

There is certainly a Brazilian-style rhythm and warmth to this one. It even opens with beach sounds and birds over Rodgers' eloquent strummed chords! However, the title doesn't fit. Rodgers and Edwards liked the city name and had mistakenly assumed it was on the coast! No matter, this instrumental is a glorious celebration of a beach on a hot day – bliss! Jay Beckenstein (from Spyro Gyra) was brought in by Kenny Lehman. He plays the lead saxophone part that is featured first, and the melody is then passed on to either George Young or Vito Rendace on the flute – Lehman doesn't remember who took the solo. The main theme is then carried on the piano before we go around again with Beckenstein, etc. There's just enough time for a third pass around the melody from Beckenstein, with the odd little lick from Rodgers, who we could have done with hearing a lot more of. He is low in the mix on rhythm guitar for most of this track, which is odd because what we can hear is perfect for the light, jazzy feel of the tune. Equally odd is that he doesn't get a solo. If he had, it would have made for an interesting contrast to the reed instrument solos. Despite the lack of Rodgers (or Edwards), this is still a lovely piece of music.

'You Can Get By'

Beginning with a 'party time' brass-heavy intro, Vandross prominently sings the chorus lines, with Edwards adding a lower harmony part and singing the verses, which suit his register well. The verse/chorus structure of the song isn't that impressive and, at just over five and a half minutes long, it would have outstayed its welcome but for the breakdown, which comes in at 2:53. Rodgers, who has been quiet up until now, steps up for a striking rhythm part over Thompson's cymbals and Figueroa's congas. The unexpected, incisive, short stabbing strings (with a slight echo treatment) at 3:20 are an exciting moment. They would use a similar dramatic effect to punctuate songs in the future, most memorably on 'Good Times'. The strings are kept in for the rest of the breakdown and make for a thrilling contrast with the rhythm section. A lick from Edwards at 3:45 leads back into the rather uninspiring chorus ad infinitum. David Friedman makes his presence felt on vibraphone during this long outro, as he does on the verses. But the best section remains that breakdown.

'Everybody Dance'

The extended (8:27) 12" version is the one to go for, with an extra 1:46 of magic. This is the version that the notes here refer to, and it can be found on the *Savoir Faire* box set. Rodgers revealed in *Le Freak* that he was the 'main writer' and effectively wrote the song alone. He explained that the song had a complicated structure, which he compensated for with the overtly simple chorus.

Rodgers told *Sound On Sound* in April 2005:

> We did it with one of my jazz-musician friends (Tom Coppola) playing clavinet, and he was not funky at all. So, when you hear that really cool solo that he plays on the song, it's actually him just playing whole notes while the rhythm is keyed by my guitar. That was our very first recording, and Bob Clearmountain (engineer) taught us how to do that. He said, 'Oh man, the keyboard player sucks! Why don't you play the rhythm Nile and just let this guy play whole notes.' I said, 'You can do that?' and he said, 'Yeah, he'll play and you'll make the rhythm for him.'

Rodgers, Edwards, Sabino and Thompson form the musical core. Eddie Martinez plays a harmony guitar solo in one of the breaks while Tom Coppola plays the aforementioned clavinet and David Friedman plays vibraphone. On vocals for the chorus are Vandross, Anderson, Gray and likely Wright. The latter gets the verses to herself, singing with a confident, assured feel, and yet there's a suggestion of youthful innocence, too.

The glory of the song is in Edwards' propulsive bass part. The vocals, too, are jubilant, squeezing every ounce of joy out of the simple words. Among those words is the key line, 'It don't mean a thing if it ain't got that swing', taken from the song of the same name recorded by the Duke Ellington Orchestra in 1932. A lovely nod back to one of the roots of the Chic sound.

The breakdown section (3:16) is one of their first and remains one of their best. It's fundamentally an Edwards solo playing around the melody line, backed only by Thompson's drums and percussive handclaps. The transition into the chorus, though, isn't as good as they would come up with in the future – no slow build-up with the other instruments coming in.

We do get another solo on the vibraphone and xylophone at 4:16, which is unusual and makes for a nice variation of the melody. A little later, at 5:30, bongos and percussion are added to the groove with a lower mixed clavinet than on the shorter album version. Rodgers, who has been subtle throughout, gets a great clipped wah-wah part at 6:29 that gives the track a different feel. Rodgers then swaps back to his rhythm guitar for a repeated melody line and a wave of choruses to the outro – the perfect ending to one of Chic's greatest songs.

Miles Showell remastered five albums for the *Chic Organisation 1977 – 1979* box set and this song was key in Rodgers' acceptance that Showell was getting the sound he wanted. Showell recalled on the Abbey Road Studios website in 2018:

> It ('Everybody Dance') had been released originally by Buddah Records and Nile and Bernard always felt that the bass end was not as strong on Atlantic's release. I can only speculate, but this was probably because Atlantic were working from a copy tape and not the original master or it could also be because Atlantic wanted to ensure they had the best chance of making it a pop hit. They could well have equalised the sound to work well on the radio. Fortunately, the Buddah tape is now in the possession of Warner Bros. Music, which means I have access to the best source.

Rodgers was thrilled to hear the song again with the bass line as they had intended it to sound.

For Chic, it was their second single. It was released in March 1978, reaching number nine in the UK and number 38 in America. Joni, Debbie and Kim Sledge (as Sister Sledge) recorded the song in 1992 for their *And Now Sledge Again* album. Rodgers appeared on the 2020 cover version of the song by Cedric Gervais and Franklin. It's a worthy spin on the song, with an updated arrangement that captures the essence of the original but also has its own special qualities, such as the flamboyant dance music style keyboards.

'Est-Ce Que C'est Chic?'

Wright sings lead on the verses, while the chorus features all the vocalists singing in unison in French. While the song has an appealing, jaunty, summery tone to it, with a very 1970s disco string arrangement, it's a lightweight composition. There is little to commend it other than the classy piano part, which stands out in the mix.

'Falling In Love With You'

This is partly a duet between Vandross and Wright. She sings the verses alone, with Vandross harmonising on the chorus. It's the first Chic ballad and sets the standard for many others to come. David Friedman plays the vibraphone that sparkles all over the intro and sets the song up. The string arrangement, which shadows the vocals, is excellent and Gloria Agostini's harp is a delight, such as at 2:40, adding emphasis to Wright's pleading delivery. Ultimately, this is a sensitive, delicate piece that never breaks into a sweat, even when Wright is at her most overwrought. It's a good song, but better ballads were to come.

'Strike Up The Band' (Edwards/Lehman/Rodgers)

Despite the usual credits, Lehman said, 'I also co-wrote 'Strike Up The Band' and I have my copyright on that.' So, we are correcting that here for him! This strident, brass-heavy statement should logically have opened the album, but not leading off with one of your hits would have been a poor decision. It certainly isn't a song to close an album either, but the remaining 'best' option – to open side two with it – was ruled out by opening that side with the other hit. So, here we find it as a kind of closing resume, their first 'this is who we are' track. This was a self-referential theme they would revisit sporadically throughout their career with the likes of 'Chic Cheer' and 'M.M.F.T.C.F.', to name just two.

It's one of the strongest tracks on the album (for the most part) with a funky clavinet part from Coppola, which calls to mind Stevie Wonder's 'Superstition'. The breakdown (2:22) gives Edwards the spotlight for a short solo, with Figueroa accompanying him on congas while Thompson sizzles on the cymbals and drums. A brass blast and a vocal exhortation of 'you've got to feel the rhythm' leads into a brief killer funk groove with Rodgers' guitar setting the tone. They should have kept that going all the way to the fade and built on it, but instead, it's a wave of choruses that fail to keep the heat up.

Norma Jean (Norma Jean Wright) (1978)

Personnel:
Norma Jean Wright: lead vocals, backing vocals
Nile Rodgers: guitar, backing vocals
Bernard Edwards: bass, backing vocals
Tony Thompson: drums, percussion
Alfa Anderson, Robin Clark, Diva Gray, David Lasley, Luther Vandross: backing vocals
Sammy Figueroa: percussion
Ray Jones: Fender Rhodes, piano
Rob Sabino, Andy Schwartz, Tom Coppola: keyboards, synth
Gene Orloff: string conductor
Kenny Lehman: woodwinds
David Friedman: tubular bells, vibraphone
George Young, Vito Rendace: flute, tenor saxophone
Alex Foster: sax solo on 'Having A Party'
Jon Faddis: trumpet
Barry Rogers: trombone
Alfred Brown: string contractor
Gloria Agostini: harp
Produced and arranged by Bernard Edwards & Nile Rodgers at Power Station, New York, in March 1978
Release date: July 1978
Label: Bearsville
Highest chart places: UK: did not chart, US: did not chart
Running time: 41:23
All songs by Edwards and Rodgers, except as noted.

Wright's solo album deal led to contractual issues that saw her having to leave Chic. At first, all was fine, and she seemed content when she spoke to David Nathan of *Classic Soul* in November 1978: '(Atlantic) heard the *Chic* album and they agreed on the deal almost straight away. I signed with them in January (1978) and we completed the album in March.' She also filled in some details on the song selection:

> There was a group effort between Nile, Bernard, and me to select the material. The guys wrote most of the material, and I co-wrote one song: 'This Is The Love'. We decided to do 'Having A Party', the Sam Cooke song, because we wanted to do an oldie but goodie and that seemed appropriate. I think the album has a lot of good things in it. I told the guys that 'So I Get Hurt Again' should be an easy thing for me to get into because I could really dig the lyrics, although I don't feel that I have a preference for ballads as opposed to up-tempo material. It all depends on the underlying message in the song and that's why I particularly like 'This Is The Love' because there's a

bit more to it than just the man-woman thing. It's got another spiritual message in there if you check it out.

While Wright's voice works well on the livelier songs, she doesn't quite convince on the ballads. Chic avoided this kind of issue on their own records – from C'est Chic onwards – by having two or three lead vocalists to pick from or using ensemble vocals. That being said, there are several very enjoyable and three essential songs on this album. The pick of them is 'Saturday', 'Sorcerer' and 'I Like Love'.

A second Norma Jean album was planned, but the plug was pulled after the release of a single, 'Hold Me Lonely Boy', in 1979. Wright told chictribute.com: 'Nile and Bernard's fee was much more than the label wished to pay.' That's a shame because the single (especially the B-side) boded well. A probable flaw for Wright, as a solo artist, was that both sides of the single featured the Chic choir plus her on the choruses. She needed to sing verses and choruses alone if she was to have any chance as a solo singer. She did, however, turn up on further Chic projects as a session vocalist.

'Saturday' (Edwards/Rodgers/Bobby Cotter)

Co-writer Bobby Cotter (miscredited as Carter) was, as noted earlier, the singer in the Big Apple Band. It's a wonderful encapsulation, musically and lyrically, of the New York disco scene. Wright gets the drudge of the working week across well in the verses before everything explodes into life in the chorus, where she is joined by the Chic choir.

The middle eight section – 'If you left it up to me' – captures the spirit of Saturday night. It's scintillating in its euphoria and power and also cues up a terrific vibraphone solo by David Friedman. It has been singled out as the standout track on the album, but there are others that hold their own equally as well. The single mix is called 'Saturday Nite', while a remix by Dimitri From Paris is 9:51 long. His work on this is outstanding, especially the prominence he gives to Edwards' awesome bass part. Then, there's the 'pop' of the vibraphone at 5:12 on Dimitri's mix, which sparkles with greater prominence. But best of all is the quite jaw-dropping section from 5:40, which is epic in terms of dynamics and drama. Dimitri strips the song to congas and handclaps before building it back up, Chic breakdown style. It's a must-hear remix.

'Having A Party' (Sam Cooke)

This pulsating cover version is the sound of a band quite literally having a party. It has a vibrant rhythm and some very E-Street band-type piano. Edwards' bass entry at 57 seconds, announcing its presence with a deep but audibly happy growl, is a wonderful moment! From then on, it's an irresistible force of nature. Wright sings with some restraint, barely able to control the musical force behind her. The solo comes from Alex Foster on saxophone, and he effectively cues up the longer outro on the extended 12" mix, which is 1:45 longer. Overall, a heart-warming, life-affirming track.

'I Believe In You' (Chris Dawkins, Norman Whitehead)
This externally written offering is the best of the ballads on the album. It doesn't quite catch fire, but the chorus has a warm, summery feel to it with the strings, piano and the terrific backing vocals. Wright sings it well enough but lacks that something special to really sell it.

'Sorcerer'
'Sorcerer' is another top-class song, marked out by some great musicianship. Rodgers' catchy guitar riff is key to the song throughout, but Friedman's great vibraphone playing and the ever-interesting lively congas of Figueroa are worthy of note. He gives the rhythm track extra punch and dynamics. The 'sorcery' is conjured up with a mix of the strings and some suitably spacey effects from a synthesiser. The chorus sees the Chic choir repeating a soft, mysterious chant of the title, with interjections from Wright. An explosion heralds the bridge, which is a Rodgers-led jam with Wright riffing around on the title, with the synth swirling around from speaker to speaker. The extended 12" mix adds another 2:14 for your pleasure, which consists of a longer outro.

'So I Get Hurt'
Another ballad which fails to connect. It's underplayed, with only Edwards maintaining interest and some nice vibraphone touches from Friedman. Other than that, and with Wright never really selling the lyrics, this is one to pass by.

'This Is The Love' (Denzil Miller, Norma Jean Wright)
This was the first song ever written by Norma, and sadly, it continues the mid-side-two slump. It's bright enough with a nice 'glow' to Wright's delivery, but it's just not good enough. However, full marks to Sammy Figueroa on congas, who is as well-judged as ever on what to play.

'I Like Love'
Thompson is outstanding on this, pushing the song along. He could have been speaking about this one, among many, when he spoke to *One Two Testing* in 1985:

> There's so much you can do with just the bass drum, snare and hi-hat. I was only allowed to play two and four, so I got my cookies off doing something on the hi-hat. I pride myself on playing 16ths on the hi-hat, but real rhythmical, not mechanical. You can do a whole bunch of groove with that. A lot of cats don't spend enough time *feeling* drums. My advice to young players is to learn time and groove – groove is all.

It's an uplifting, sweet, positive song and a real hidden sleeper classic in the Chic catalogue. A twisting riff by Rodgers opens it, followed closely by Edwards' bass and Thompson's drums. The backing singers come in for the chorus, which is simply the title repeated over and over – a joyous affirmation. Wright is superb, too, taking the verses alone, while the choruses are almost hypnotic.

Musically, it has so much else going on apart from the core instruments of bass, guitar and keyboards – congas, strings, Fender Rhodes, brass – all adding to the details. The breakdown (at 3:02) is always an intrinsically great part of any Chic song, and this is perhaps the best of them all. It shimmers and grooves with a brilliance that is quite breathtaking. Rodgers' chucka-chucka guitar (and at least one other higher rhythm guitar) opens it, accompanied only by Thompson's bass drum, sizzling cymbals and some distant keyboards. The strings come back in playing the song's melody over and over before the Chic choir begin repeating the song's title. Thompson's quick fill sets up the outro, which is chorus after chorus. It leaves you breathless in wonder and it remains one of the finest songs the Organisation ever recorded.

Related Tracks

'Hold Me Lonely Boy'

The A-side of Wright's 1979 single. Ray Jones was credited specifically on piano and Sammy Figueroa on percussion (in CD notes). It's a good song, but it lacks that 'something' to mark it out as special. This is largely down to the very uninspiring chorus, even though Jean is bolstered by the harmony vocals from the backing singers. The verses are less repetitive and have an airy feel, with the strings working well. The best part, though, is the instrumental break, with Figueroa to the fore. An extended version (5:16) was included in the *Savoir Faire* box set.

'High Society'

This was the B-side of the single. For me, it's the better song of the two, with a catchy hook and chorus and a vibrant string arrangement. The verses remind me of the tempo and intonation on 'I Got Protection' on the later *Real People* album. Figueroa gets a percussion solo, which is unique in the Chic canon. He plays at least three overlaid parts in what is a masterclass of percussion work. The song was featured as a 12" mix on the re-release of the album and the *Savoir Faire* set.

Following the release of *Chic* and *Norma Jean,* matters came to a head between Turtle Productions and Rodgers and Edwards. Kenny Lehman had to make a difficult choice:

> I was going to be part of Chic, obviously, but then my partners (Turtle) didn't offer the option on the contract, which was ridiculous in my

opinion. So Nile and Bernard decided to go off on their own and I was caught between them on one side and Turtle Productions on the other. I decided to wait and see what happened in the meeting between Nile, Bernard, the attorneys and Turtle Productions. At that meeting, Nile and Bernard said to me, 'Kenny, you can be part of Chic; we are going to produce on our own', but I didn't like that idea because Turtle had a track record and I didn't know what the future of Chic was going to be. So I stayed with Turtle and was no longer in the good graces of Nile and Bernard.

Chic toured in support of their debut. An inspiration for the look of the band was Roxy Music, whom Rodgers saw live and had a lightbulb moment over their stage presentation – the band in suits and the female backing singers. The material for the set was drawn from their debut, as well as the yet-to-be-released *C'est Chic*. Their first official date was at Casanova's Nightclub in Atlantic City on 14 April 1978. The tour worked around the US, finally finishing in New York on 24 July.

The core band was made up of Rodgers, Edwards and Thompson. They also took out ten other musicians/vocalists for what was their largest-ever live lineup. Sabino opted out, going with the Simms Brothers instead, so Thompson suggested Ray Jones for keyboards. He duly came in for the tour and subsequently stayed on to play on the records, too. Norma Jean Wright was there on lead vocals, backed by Luther Vandross and Alfa Anderson.

There was also a string section, with the four-piece unit being Marianne Carroll, Cheryl Hong, Karen Milne and Claire Bergman. The latter did not stay on to record with Chic. Milne told David Nathan of *Classic Soul* in 1979 how she came on board via an ad in her apartment building: 'I saw the ad and, at first, I wasn't going to bother. (But) I'd been in New York for three months, and I figured I'd just take a chance! It's definitely been a challenge because it's a whole different energy. I mean not playing classical music and not having to wear long black dresses!'

To further fill out the sound, they recruited Jean Fineberg and Ellen Seeling as the brass section. Fineberg outlines her background:

I play tenor saxophone; I have an alto as well, but I primarily play tenor. I have played music all my life. I started piano when I was six and then I went through recorder, then flute, and then, when I was in college, I played guitar and sang folk songs. I came out to Berkeley, California, from New York, and I got into a rock band that would play Jethro Tull music because I was a flute player. But I got tired of that and I wanted to play more rock 'n' roll. So I got a saxophone and I took a bunch of lessons and then I got in a band in New York. I was in this band called Ecstasy, Passion & Pain and the keyboard player was Ray Jones; he got us the audition that led to us joining Chic. Tony (Thompson) was also in that band.

Trumpeter Ellen Seeling's background was as a jazz player.

> I went to New York around 1976 and played with a bunch of acts. I almost didn't do the Chic audition because, at that point, we (she and Jean Fineberg) had already played with some big acts and I didn't feel like I wanted to audition for anybody. But we went for the audition, which was in a rehearsal space. I am speculating, but I think because they had an all-female string section, they wanted the same thing for a horn section. If that was the case, we were pretty much the only game in town. We already had a track record, so they had heard about us and we got the gig. We were the horn section on stage, and then when we went into the studio, they expanded it.

Rehearsals revealed that it was Edwards who called the shots. Seeling said that 'Bernard was just uncompromising. I remember that, at rehearsals and on stage, he would sometimes get on at Tony about what he was playing. The disco thing was that repeated hi-hat sound and the bass drum, and Tony would deviate from that once in a while because pretty much any drummer would. He caught flak from Bernard whenever he tried that.' She was impressed by Edwards' playing: 'Although the harmonic structure was pretty static, the basslines were challenging because they were so fast. Most bass players will play with all four/five fingers, but Bernard would use his index finger like a pick. He would put his index finger between his thumb and third finger and he would play like that. I am not a fan of disco music, but I would say that was the best rhythm section in disco by far.'

Rodgers, she could see, was a very original player: 'Nile's approach was very unique. I still hear commercials on TV that use the same approach, the rhythm guitar thing that Nile developed.'

The strings and brass being all female made for an interesting dynamic. Fineberg feels it was entirely deliberate:

> I think they chose female string and horn players as part of the show. They gave us money to buy clothing. But we are not dress-wearing women, so they had to work out how to dress us in a way that looked right without asking us to put on dresses, which we wouldn't do. So we ended up going to Bergdorf Goodman, which is a very expensive store on Fifth Avenue in Manhattan, and we bought matching white wool suits. Then they sent us to a place where they had their shirts custom-made and we had some button-down shirts. Then I remember wearing hats. They thought it would be cool to have the string players dressed very feminine, which they didn't mind, and then us dressed in suits and hats. I think that added to the image and we were happy.

The early tour dates saw an unforeseen problem. The debut album cover suggested that the whistle-blowing duo might be the twin lead vocalists. While the sound of the band was right, the look, with Wright alone on lead vocals, was not. After the first run of dates, they fixed the imbalance. They looked for a second, lighter-skinned lead vocalist. Clare Bathen was auditioned, but although a fine vocalist, she was felt to be not so good a dancer.

Instead, in came a good friend of Wright's – Luci Martinez (shortened to Martin), a Bronx-born Puerto Rican. That was a curious, although welcome, decision because they had Alfa Anderson already there in waiting. Perhaps the feeling was that her voice wouldn't blend so well with Wright's on lead lines. The now 13-piece lineup didn't last as Wright soon left. She had been offered a deal with Bearsville, which Rodgers has said he and Edwards brokered. With Bearsville under the auspices of Warner Bros., who were connected to Atlantic, it meant she had not gone far. Wright believed she could have a solo career and remain part of Chic, but contractual complications prevented this. Anderson stepped forward to replace Wright, and thus, the ultimate Chic frontline of her and Martin was in place.

The tour saw the band playing to large audiences wherever they appeared. Seeling says:

> The smallest venues we did were 20,000 seaters. We were usually the opener, but there would be several acts on the bill; we opened for The O'Jays, Earth, Wind and Fire, Evelyn Champagne King, Parliament and Bootsy's Rubber Band. Our set was very choreographed. I was used to playing a lot more than we actually got to play with Chic, but we had to be on stage with them the whole time. When we weren't playing, we tried to look engaged. Jean (Fineberg) is a good dancer, showperson and performer. I'm not so much, so that was a little painful for me.

Each show opened with 'Strike Up The Band' and was innovative for the time because the band would start the song off-stage. The rest of the setlist is conjecture, but obviously, the hit singles were featured. There is not much out there to see of the band in this era. An *American Bandstand* performance sees Wright miming with Luci Martin to the two singles. A recording of the *Midnight Special* performance in 1978 is a must-see. After a great performance of 'Le Freak', we get 'Everybody Dance' with Anderson's silky lead vocals. This is the best recording of the song, with her on lead instead of Norma Jean Wright. There is also footage on YouTube (via Matt Quigley) of 'Dance, Dance, Dance', which is dated as 1977 but is actually 1978. It's great sound quality (although the video is only fair) and you get to hear Martin and Anderson performing the vocals. There is also a 3:23 promo video of 'Everybody Dance', which shows the band complete with the strings and brass section and gives an indication of how they set up on stage.

A highlight for Seeling and Fineberg was 'Sao Paolo', with Seeling recalling that it was 'a little Brazilian tune. That was one thing I did get to actually play on a good amount. That was a challenge to get up in front of 20,000 people.'

Fineberg loved the song because 'I do enjoy performing. We would get up in front of the band and we would play it. It got a really great response from the audience, and then all of a sudden, it was dropped from the show and we didn't know why.'

To fill out the setlist, Seeling says that they 'were doing some of the new material that wound up on the second album. They were probably road-testing it to see if it got any response from the audience.' Rodgers and Edwards treated the band well. Seeling says: 'We were like side players. Often, bands would put side musicians in cheaper accommodation, but Chic always put everyone up in the same hotels, so that was nice. But we didn't socialise with them, really. Mostly, it was Nile, Bernard and Tony that hung out together.'

The band were augmented by Sammy Figueroa on percussion for some shows: 'We did a bunch of concerts in New York and we played LA. I couldn't do all of them because, at the time, I was working with Eric Clapton and then Average White Band for about four years. Otherwise, I would have done more shows.'

Despite the inter-band harmony and the sell-out shows, the lineup was not to last and it was the brass duo of Seeling and Fineberg who were dispensed with. Fineberg recalls the end:

> *C'est Chic* was out by the time we went on the big European tour. I know we did America and Brazil, too. After Brazil, we were supposed to do Mexico and Nile and Bernard flew ahead separately. We (the band) were in Venezuela and thought we were getting the plane to go to Mexico, but the plane went to New York. So we talked to the Road Manager and he said, 'Oh, Mexico is cancelled, but you'll get paid anyway.' It was strange; gigs get cancelled – we knew that, but we didn't know until we got on the plane. Everybody was disappointed and offended that nobody had told us. So we voiced those feelings on the plane and the Road Manager told them (Edwards and Rodgers). When we were back in New York, they called us into the office. Nile and Bernard started ripping us apart, saying, 'We heard all the things you said on the plane.' They were going on and on, so I piped up and I said, 'Are you firing us?' and they said, 'Yes', so we walked out and that was that. I have fond feelings about Nile now, and he may have fond feelings about us, but we got fired from that band.

Seeling feels that the actual root of the problem was that 'they couldn't afford a horn section anymore.' Looking back, she feels that 'it was a great experience for me, something different to the other things I had done. They were aware that they were racially different from other disco bands at the time, and I think their audiences were largely white. I think there might have been some tension about that.'

C'est Chic (Chic) (1978)

Personnel:
Nile Rodgers: guitar, backing vocals
Bernard Edwards: bass, lead vocals on 'Happy Man' and 'Sometimes You Win'
Tony Thompson: drums, percussion
Alfa Anderson: lead vocals on 'Le Freak', 'I Want Your Love', 'At Last I Am Free' and 'Sometimes You Win', backing vocals
Diva Gray: lead vocals on 'Le Freak', backing vocals
Luci Martin: vocals
Sammy Figueroa: percussion
Ray Jones: Fender Rhodes, keyboards
Rob Sabino: clavinet, electric piano, acoustic piano on 'Le Freak'
Andy Schwartz: piano on 'At Last I Am Free'
Cheryl Hong, Marianne Carroll, Karen Milne: the Chic strings
Gene Orloff: concertmaster
Jose Rossy: tubular bells on 'I Want Your Love'
Jon Faddis, Ellen Seeling: trumpet
Jean Fineberg, Alex Foster: saxophone
Barry Rogers: trombone
Produced and arranged by Bernard Edwards & Nile Rodgers at Power Station, New York, between April and July 1978
Release date: 11 August 1978
Label: Atlantic
Highest chart places: UK: 2, USA: 4
Running time: 41:23
All songs by Edwards and Rodgers.

The band broke off from touring to lay down material in the studio. Norma Jean Wright doesn't appear in the credits, which is puzzling because when talking to David Nathan for *Classic Soul* in November 1978, she told him that she was 'finishing off the second Chic album (*C'est Chic*) and doing background work on a Sister Sledge album, which Nile and Bernard are producing.' So, she *was* either there for the sessions and uncredited, or her background vocals were only kept for the simultaneously recorded *We Are Family*.

On the vocal front, we have the start of the dream team – Alfa Anderson and Luci Martin. The duo spoke to *Wax Poetics* in the summer of 2015. Interviewer A. D. Amorosi reported that Anderson described her Chic sound as piercing, clear and smooth, adding that 'I didn't have what people thought of as a heavy soulful voice.' Martin said that she started her singing career accidentally when she auditioned for *Hair*. 'I was going to be a chorus girl, dancing. My ambition wasn't to be a singer. The producers asked me to do 'Aquarius', liked it, and I got the job.' Martin then recalled how she was recruited for Chic at a party attended by Rodgers, Edwards and Thompson. 'I knew Tony from Queens, and we joked about the neighbourhood the whole time until Nile asked me if I'd heard 'Dance, Dance, Dance'. No, disco wasn't my thing.' It was then that Martin hit them with a curve ball, telling Rodgers and Edwards that one of the notes in the 'ba-ba-ba-ba' section was incorrect – 'if you're following the chord, the next note should be a half-step down.' The trio left the room, returned, and told Martin that she was in. 'In what?' she asked!

The importance of strings to the Chic sound was firmly endorsed for this album with the arrival of the celebrated Chic strings. Percussion-wise, Sammy Figueroa was the main man and was fully involved in the rhythm tracks. He says:

> Tony (Thompson) and I were really good friends. I was so used to doing studio work that they trusted my instincts and how I felt about what to play. They never told me what to do; there was nothing written for percussion. Nile never said, 'I want you to play a shaker' or whatever. He just said, 'Go in there, do whatever you want.' So, I did whatever felt right on each track. I would sometimes say, 'Hey, I don't feel that this song needs percussion; just keep the groove as it is'. And they would be shocked when I said that, but they knew that my instincts were right. My whole thing was just to make the groove bigger. Most of the time, I would create a rhythm with just woodblocks, tambourine and a cowbell. Tony Thompson would be playing a groove, and for me, it was about enhancing the groove rather than overindulging in your ego.

Figueroa commented on Rodgers and Edwards' style in the studio:

> They worked together perfectly. Bernard was the one who had that master-groove thing; he was the one who laid down the foundation with his basslines. Nile is a rhythm guy, you know, not especially a soloist like a blues guitar player like Stevie Ray Vaughan. That groove Nile plays on the songs made them famous. Now, everybody copies those lines.

'I Want Your Love' was nearly not recorded by Chic. The original intention was to record 'He's The Greatest Dancer', with Sister Sledge getting 'I Want Your Love'. The decision was reversed, although Kathy Sledge has claimed she can still hear their voices on the backing vocals of 'I Want Your Love'. In fact, both albums (*C'est Chic* and *We Are Family*) were recorded at the same time! The basic tracks for both albums were recorded in Studio B at Power Station over four days, while the string and brass overdubs were recorded in the larger Studio A. The challenge of recording two albums with the same crew of musicians meant punishing round-the-clock schedules for Rodgers, Edwards and the core band. They worked fast; it is known that 'Le Freak's backing tracks (guitar, bass, drums and keyboards) were done in just two hours! Three keyboard players are credited overall on the album. It hasn't been explicitly stated how the contracts were worked out, but Andy Schwartz (real name Andrew Barrett) was definitely hired as a session player behind Sabino and Jones.

The brass section recorded parts for four albums in one session! Jean Fineberg says that:

> The strings were recorded completely separately from the horns in the studio. We had the charts, but very little was known. Just go into the studio, play this and play that. Nile and Bernard might say, 'Oh, play this note shorter or don't play this note.' I don't know if we even knew the names of the tunes or what the album was going to be called. But the horn lines were fun to play; they were good lines. We were definitely musicians for hire. I am sure they had the plan in their heads, but they didn't share it with us. There was a definite separation between the principals – Nile and Bernard – and then the second layers of the female singers and then the horns and the strings. It wasn't like one big happy community band, although I am also *not* saying it was unhappy. Nile and Bernard had a vision; they were very professional and they knew exactly what they were gonna do. As far as they were concerned, they and the female singers were the band.

Ellen Seeling adds:

> The guys put down the basics, then they did a bunch of pads and electronic stuff. They put the vocals on last. There were a number of tracks that did not include horns at all, but for the few we did play, it worked out great. In fact, we did all the horn parts in one three-hour session for all those albums. They weren't very involved; they weren't difficult. I mean, it's possibly the simplest stuff I have ever recorded. We just knocked them off pretty fast. We didn't know the parts were going to show up on other albums. They had the basic tracks for each tune when we did our session. I don't think most of our parts were harmonised; we just played in octaves.

Regarding fees for the musicians, Fineberg says:

> The way it worked back then was we got a certain fee for the session, which was like a couple of hundred dollars. Then, any mechanical or writers' royalties go to the band or the composer. However, there are other royalties called New Use, which is when a song is used in a movie, television, overseas, or anything but the record sales here. All the people on the records got those royalties, so we got considerable royalties from New Use.

Seeling adds: 'I think the guys got paid double scale because they were the most in-demand studio players in New York at that time.'

The album was topped off with an extravagant cover photograph taken by Joel Brodsky, which captured the core five band members in a room of a curiously empty but opulent house. The view behind them out into the gardens enhances the feel of luxury. The track titles are listed below the photograph, which is a clever nod to the past when this was more common on covers and also gives more impact to the titles. The back cover is equally as good, with Brodsky's superb photograph of the five in the corner of a room of likely the same house. Both front and rear images are a perfect fit for the music, capturing the style of the band.

The first UK edition of this album was called *Tres Chic.* It added 'Everybody Dance' and 'Dance, Dance, Dance' to the running order (one on the end of each side), which were welcome additions for UK purchasers, although affecting the integrity of the original album. This misstep was compounded by a different and dreadful cover image of a woman wrapped around a neon tube against the backdrop of a city at night! But the 'proper' *C'est Chic* is at the top of the summit as Chic's best album. The band were on such a roll, however, that their next band record would join it at the top.

'Chic Cheer'

The opening audience noise is sampled from Jac Holzman's *Authentic Sound Effects Volume 3,* which came out on Elektra in 1964. It makes for a good intro, implying a live performance, with Rodgers' cheeky guitar lick punctuated by Thompson's cymbals. It builds nicely from there into the vocals chanting 'chic, chic, chic' and then the command of 'everybody sway'. From there, it's a catchy riff from Rodgers with a harmony rhythm guitar part, accompanied by a taut backing track. But this gets rather repetitive, the formula lacking interest or panache. There is no lead vocalist either, and the ensemble vocals merely contribute to the overall problem that there is little that impresses and leaves you wanting more. There are many fans who love this song, but for me, it's average at best.

Edwards remixed the song when it was re-released as a single in 1984. He removed the crowd noises and gave the song more punch and dynamics. The song really does come to life more, although the drums are far too loud. Nonetheless, this is well worth seeking out.

'Le Freak'

This is one of Chic's best-known songs and the biggest-selling single in Atlantic's history. The best version is the full-length album take, which is nearly two minutes longer than the single. It's the album version we will be referencing. The song's inception came on New Year's Eve 1977 when Rodgers and Edwards were refused entrance into Studio 54 despite being invited by the headliner on the night, Grace Jones. Back home, they got the funky riff down quickly, ending it with a hook of 'Fuck off' – the words from the doorman as he closed the door on them! However, they changed the lyric to 'Freak out', and the rest is history. In the lyric, they reference 'Stompin' At The Savoy', which was written by Edgar Sampson back in 1933. Studio 54 also gets a mention, with the invite to 'Come on down to 54'.

The song opens with a 'one, two' before we are thrown straight into the chorus, a guaranteed way to open a song with a bang! In fact, we get several choruses adorned by the choir. Anderson and Diva Gray harmonise on the verses with an almost nonchalant vibe. Rodgers told *Sound On Sound* in April 2005 that 'Alfa's voice is instantly recognisable to me by the way she sings 'I'm sure you'll be amazed'. The word 'amazed' is kinda flat and very Alfa Anderson, a cool thing that we used to love. Still, 'Le Freak' is mainly about the music. There's probably more playing than singing.' Thompson's big bass drum sound was achieved, said Rodgers in the same interview, by 'overloading the live echo chamber, which was the bathroom at the Power Station.' You can hear it at its most intense following each chorus vocal.

For the breakdown with the choir singing 'I say Freak!', engineer Bob Clearmountain used studio trickery when recording the handclaps using an echo chamber. By using reverse reverb, it meant that the echo came before the clap!

The combination of Rodgers' euphoric rhythm guitars (there are at least two interweaving rhythm parts) and the pulsing bass by Edwards is terrific, and as usual, there is the cinematic drama of the string arrangement. In spite of that, the arrangement has a sparse feel at times – there is little or no percussion evident and the keyboards are equally low in the mix.

The best section comes after the 'Now freak' exclamation at 2:44. We get an interlude that rises and rises in power until, with nowhere else to go, it drops off with a bass lick from Edwards, connecting it into another verse. It's just tremendous! The outro is over a minute of choruses with one key attention-grabbing addition – Thompson gets to play an explosive fill, initially at 4:55 and then again at 5:11.

The single got to number one in America. It had three separate runs at the top, broken by Neil Diamond and Barbra Streisand's 'You Don't Bring Me Flowers' and the Bee Gees' 'Too Much Heaven'. On 21 March 2018, the song was selected for preservation in the National Recording Registry by the Library of Congress as being 'culturally, historically or artistically significant.'

Dimitri From Paris borrows 'Chic Cheer' for a new intro on his mix, which otherwise isn't significantly better than the original.

'Savoir Faire'

An instrumental akin to 'Sao Paolo', Rodgers' jazzy guitar solo is one he picked out as his best. 'It's still my favourite solo,' he told Gene Santoro for *Downbeat* in September 1985, 'because it was the most complete for me. I started the melody with chords, then moved into the jazzy stuff. It was really emotional, and from a compositional point of view, it's one of the best things I've ever played.'

It's a breezy piece of work that worked well as an opener for side two of the album. It is, for the most part, a vehicle for Rodgers, who is superb. He stands out in the mix, which heavily features the strings, which switch between a multi-layered approach to the main melody line and lighter accents when the mix drops down for the more laid-back sections. There's an excellent piano line in the mix, too, which occasionally 'pops' out. As great as Rodgers is on this, it might have benefited from that piano line being mixed a little higher.

'Happy Man'

Edwards sings lead on this lyrical affirmation of his lifestyle at the time. He is happy 'spreadin' all my love around the place' (meaning the world) and happy 'hanging out all night with the jet set'. The chorus asserts that 'the world is my home', so it seems Edwards (and likely Rodgers, too) was coping well with the touring/recording lifestyle. No insight into domestic circumstances is mentioned. Lyrically, this is the positive flip side of 'Real People', by which time the lifestyle had worn thin.

Anderson and Martin provide supporting vocals to lift things up in parts of the chorus, but Edwards handles the verses alone. It's an exuberant song and the pulsating rhythm track gives it a real driving quality. Rodgers gets an excellent, tasteful short solo, which is the bridge between the two halves of the track. Edwards is quite magnificent on bass; his main riff has echoes of the one he plays on 'Everybody Dance'. The wandering bass runs he launches into from around the 2:50 mark are a highlight of the extended instrumental outro. It's not a great song, but it's enjoyable enough for the warm, happy performance.

'I Want Your Love'

Among the several songs which are among the best the Organisation have ever recorded, this one is my personal favourite. Everything that is great about their records could be summed up in this one song, which never seems to lose its freshness and impact. The album version is the best, being nearly three and a half minutes longer than the single. Therefore, it's the album version we will be referencing. If the lyrics sound heartfelt, it's because Rodgers meant every word, as exemplified in 2000's *Very Best Of Chic* notes: '(It) was about a real-life affair I was involved in, where I was going out with one girl, but I wanted to go out with her best friend.' The chorus vocals ache with unrequited love, but it's the verses which have the emotional heart, with Anderson delivering a supreme performance: 'Just one chance and I will show you love, like no other two steps above.'

There are so many aspects to this song that define it. Aside from the catchy rhythm and guitar melody, there is the ever-present tubular bells and horn section, all perfectly balanced by the strings. The instrumental break at 3:23 is overwhelming. Rodgers' guitars keep the tension going while the strings soar and swoop from loss to euphoria in a dizzying rush. There's a lovely part here at 3:57 where it escalates and the brass comes in to play the same melody lines as the strings. It's simply stunning! Rodgers leads the way out from here into the breakdown (4:29), which drops right down to Rodgers' chucka-chucka rhythm parts, with Edwards and Thompson also keeping the rhythm going. Sabino's acoustic piano has been in the mix throughout, but his piano is most evident as they come out of the breakdown. He plays the melody line slowly and very deliberately and it creates such a strong contrast to the rest of the backing track. More from the brass and a heady instrumental whirl lead inevitably into the chorus/outro. The song reinforced that Chic were more than just a 'disco' act and was a smash hit single in its edited form in the UK (number four) and in America (number seven).

There is an 8:34 remix by Dimitri From Paris, which is even more thrilling than the original. Joni, Debbie and Kim Sledge (as Sister Sledge) recorded the song in 1992 for their *And Now Sledge Again* album.

'At Last I Am Free'

This is an old Rodgers song (predating Chic) that he originally wrote following a Black Panthers demonstration in Central Park, New York. The political lyrics were reworked with a new theme about moving on in love, courtesy of Edwards.

There's a beautiful, weightless feel to this sublime ballad. Anchoring the heart of the song is Edwards' steady bassline, Thompson's slow pulse drums and a lovely piano part from Andy Schwartz. Rodgers plays chiming guitar licks around the trio while the strings add deft, sensitive touches.

Anderson takes the lead on the verses and the Chic choir softly sing the chorus, adding to the shimmering musical top notes from Rodgers and the strings. The exception to this comes with the chorus at 3:28, which Anderson sings alone. It has the effect of suggesting she has 'made it' out of whatever predicament she is in. From there, it's repeated choir choruses all the way to the end. Schwartz is quite delightful in this section. His piano part is a stately, attractive take on the song's melody. Everything dies down until there's only Schwartz left playing and he carries the tune out in fine style.

It's the best of the Chic ballads and among their best songs. They get so much out of comparatively little in the arrangement and it's an absolutely masterful piece of work.

'Sometimes You Win'

This duet (largely speaking) between Anderson and Edwards has the similarly warm, Latin feel of 'Sao Paolo'. They trade vocal lines on the verses, with Anderson handling lead vocals on the choruses alone, along with backing vocals. The brass section, which unexpectedly enter at 3:07, offer a melodic diversion, but it isn't a great fit. This section would have been better handled as a guitar or piano break, which would have kept the mood going. The backing track features some nice Fender Rhodes and vibes in the mix, but overall, this pleasant song borders on being filler.

'(Funny) Bone'

An unsatisfactory, closing 'fun' track. The brass are back, with Sabino adding punchy clavinet for extra measure. Along with some looped party sounds now and then, it's entirely down to the brass and strings to add colour to what is a rhythmic but essentially dull backing track.

'Bone' was a Rodgers/Edwards nickname for Thompson, who has the final words of advice before signing off with a 'ciao'! An outtake version was included in the *Savoir Faire* box set. This is a run-through of the backing track by Rodgers, Edwards, Sabino and Thompson. It's inessential and merely highlights that more would be needed to make this work.

We Are Family (Sister Sledge) (1979)

Personnel:
Debbie Sledge, Joni Sledge, Kathy Sledge and Kim Sledge: lead vocals (see songs for credits)
Nile Rodgers: guitar
Bernard Edwards: bass
Tony Thompson: drums, percussion
Alfa Anderson, Norma Jean Wright, Diva Gray, David Lasley, Luther Vandross: harmony and backing vocals
Sammy Figueroa: percussion
Ray Jones: keyboards, Fender Rhodes
Rob Sabino: clavinet, piano
Andy Schwartz: piano
Cheryl Hong, Marianne Carroll, Karen Milne: the Chic strings
Gene Orloff: concertmaster
Jon Faddis, Ellen Seeling: trumpet
Jean Fineberg, Alex Foster: saxophone
Barry Rogers: trombone
Produced and arranged by Bernard Edwards and Nile Rodgers at Power Station, New York, between April and July 1978
Release date: 22 January 1979
Label: Cotillion
Running time: 43:56
Highest chart places: UK: 7, US: 3
All songs by Edwards and Rodgers.

Rodgers told *Sound On Sound* in April 2005 why he and Edwards elected to work with Sister Sledge:

> Jerry Greenberg (President of Atlantic Records) said, 'You guys can do so great for yourselves. Can you do it for other people, too?' We didn't know we could. We just said we could. We chose Sister Sledge. You see, we kept thinking that if we worked with a big star and we got a hit, we'd be obscured by the big star and nobody would know what we did. But if we took somebody who was unknown and put them on the map, then everybody would say, 'Wow, these guys are star makers and hit makers!'

Sister Sledge, for their part, were initially 'apprehensive' of working with the duo. Kathy Sledge was sold on the deal, she told James Hardy of *Popmatters* in February 2019, when she heard a certain something: 'Jerry Greenberg told them (Rodgers and Edwards) that we fly like birds of a feather. That ended up in the song. I thought: 'They wrote that just for us?' They meant business and it showed in everything they did to bring that album together.'

The Sisters' previous albums and singles were good. Best known in the UK was 'Mama Never Told Me', which reached number 20 in the singles chart in 1973. It was, and is, a catchy song with a strong earworm of a chorus and a confident, strong vocal from Kathy Sledge. Still, they had yet to break out big and it was going to come via Rodgers and Edwards and a whole new way of working. Kathy explained to *Heart 80s* in 2019 that Rodgers and Edwards 'believed in spontaneity, so I wasn't allowed to hear 'We Are Family' until it was time to record it.'

Joni told Alex Petridis for *The Guardian* in April 2012 that the vocal sessions were 'fun but challenging. Bernard and my sister Debbie were both musical geniuses when it came to harmony, chording, things like that, and in the studio, they were like, 'Grrr!' Nile was the mediator. One day in the studio, they both walked out, and Nile was like, 'Alright, okay, everybody take a break. I'm going to talk to Debbie.' They would bicker and he was the vicar!' The control which the duo had over the whole recording process nearly came to a head with a dispute over one line in 'He's The Greatest Dancer': 'My crème de la crème, please take me home'. While Rodgers insisted it was no reflection of their personal standards, the sisters were not happy at the suggestion of impropriety. The line wasn't changed and the sisters backed down.

The album was recorded at the same time as *C'est Chic,* but there is one curious difference – both Norma Jean Wright and David Lasley (from the debut *Chic* album) are featured on *We Are Family* but *not* on *C'est Chic.* This oddity has never been explained. Their presence among the usual coterie of Chic backing and harmony singers is a big factor in this sounding like a Chic record. The sisters' actual involvement is kept to lead vocals only, with their only confirmed backing vocals being on the title track. Debbie Sledge, in particular, was against the use of the Chic Choir at first, pointing out that the Sisters could sing leads, harmonies and backing vocals themselves. However, Rodger's and Edwards' decision to use their regular singers stood. Although Debbie (for one) was impressed by the results, the sisters' belief in their own vocal qualities didn't go away and this led to them getting their own way for the follow-up album.

It's an extremely strong album, one of the very best from the Organisation, with a well-balanced song selection, including four out-and-out classics in 'He's The Greatest Dancer', 'Lost In Music', 'Thinking Of You' and 'We Are Family'. 'Dancer' was originally going to be on *C'est Chic,* while 'I Want Your Love' was intended for *We Are Family.* In truth, either could have fitted on both albums. Even the cover, which shows the sisters elegantly draped over the furniture in an opulent room, looks like a room in the same house Chic are in on the *C'est Chic* cover, further exemplifying that both albums can be viewed as two halves of the same body of work. When the record came out, the double punch of *We Are Family* and *C'est Chic* was so potent. The two records, plus the associated singles, catapulted Chic into the big time.

'He's The Greatest Dancer'

A great opening track which sets the gold standard for the album. It opens with Thompson's drums, swiftly followed by Rodgers' fluid guitar line, a riff that is the melodic anchor of the song. The rhythm itself is tight but loose, which comes from Rodgers, whose guitar gives the song an almost jaunty feel. He augments his defining rhythm line with a second guitar line, playing harmonic licks.

Kathy recalled to *Heart 80s* in 2019 that Rodgers and Edwards had her record the vocal 'line for line – 'One night in a disco' – cut.' So, what we hear is a 'comped' best version assembled from all of her vocal cuts. However, Kathy is every bit as great as the backing track. She may be 'comped', but her delivery is superb, showcasing a soft rasp to her voice that suits the lyrics perfectly. You can hear her pleasure as she sings the sticking point line 'my crème de la crème, please take me home', for example. The pinnacle is surely the audible relish she gets in the delivery of 'Fiorucci' at 2:28! The strings come into their own, too, especially with the dramatic sweeps on the bridge/breakdown at 3:41, where they are the melodic lead over Thompson's drums and cymbals. Rodgers leads the way back for more choruses and an instrumental glide to the outro.

There is a remix by Dimitri From Paris that is well worth listening to. It was the first single off the album, reaching the dizzy heights of number six in Britain and number nine in America.

'Lost In Music'

This outstanding song thrills me today as much as it did when I first heard it. Rodgers told the Glastonbury Festival crowd in 2013: 'Me and Bernard Edwards, we used to talk every night on the phone, and we'd ask each other, 'Well what the hell are you up to?', and he would say, 'I'm lost in music', and I would say, 'Me too'.'

It's an amazing vocal from the late Joni Sledge and remains a tribute to her talents. She described the song to Alex Petridis for *The Guardian* in 2012 as akin to 'being in a trance.' In the same interview, Debbie revealed that she wasn't impressed when she first heard it: 'I, in my ignorance, said to Nile: 'Well, I think it's too repetitive.' He just looked at Bernard, but Joni sang that song and the lyrics were so reflective of her personality. She's like that to this day: it's all of our passion, but she's really focused, she's all up in that music. The words are about determination, not giving up, so they kind of fitted where we were at the time.'

I am referencing the longer album version here because we get a minute and a half of extra joy over the single mix. The intro is relatively understated for the Organisation, introducing the rhythm and melody and building up, as more components are added, to the opening chorus. It's already dripping with drama as Rodgers' chattering guitar line soars. The ensemble vocal has a 'distanced' tone that calls to mind the similar feel of the chorus to 'Spacer'.

The backing track is brilliant, albeit slightly reined in. The effect is that Joni is not in any way overshadowed by the music. It fully complements her verse vocals and the Chic choir choruses. Joni scat sings some ad-libbed vocal at 3:35, including the 'la, da, da, da, dah' at 3:39 that would go on to become an essential mesmerising feature of the wonderful 1984 remix. The last minute or so is chorus after chorus. All you can do is be overwhelmed by just how lushly fabulous it is with the powerhouse vocals, the strings and those delicious lyrical licks from Rodgers.

It was the third and final single from the album. This masterpiece only reached number 17 in the UK and didn't even chart in America – it deserved to chart much higher.

The song got a new lease of life in August 1984 with a thrilling remix by Rodgers. This extended 6:38 version featured brief guest cameo vocals from Simon Le Bon and Andy Taylor at 3:38 (the words 'melody, melody', etc). In the same section, Joni scats the 'la la da da dah' refrain hypnotically, with the earworm piano part right up the mix. It's stunning! The song got to number four in the UK, and rightly so. An underwhelming 'Sure Is Pure' remix hit the charts again in 1993, but the song's innate catchy quality was still enough to see it reach number 14 in the UK. An outstanding mix by Dimitri From Paris, which is 7:51 long, was included in the *Savoir Faire* box set.

'Somebody Loves Me'

This ballad acts as a respite between two of the more full-on 'big' songs. It opens with beautifully lush strings, which are the perfect setting for Kathy's lead vocal. She is excellent at delivering the reflective lyrics. The stately rhythm of the song is offset beautifully by the shimmering strings and the piano melody, which help to give the song a light, airy feel. The vocal arrangement is terrific, especially how Kathy sings with the backing vocalists in the choruses. Her voice punctuates their almost ethereal refrain and it works a treat. Her best moment comes when she hits the high notes at 4:16 on the outro. It's just delightful. While this is a good song, it lacks a little something, such as a Rodgers solo, to give it that extra quality or depth. In my opinion, Diana Ross would have loved to cover this song, given the chance.

'Thinking Of You'

Kathy picked it out to *Popmatters* as her favourite track:

> Lyrically, it's just so sweet. And it has such a breezy flow. I think of it as a groove love song. With some songs, the second you hear them, they lift you, and Nile's guitar, during the intro, immediately takes you there. Right away, I thought to myself, 'I'm gonna enjoy singing this.' I remember it being two in the morning when I recorded it, and I was feeling good. That's why I go up the scale at the end. I was smiling because it made me happy and people listening to it can feel that, too.

Kathy is spot on – this is an enormous feel-good song that hits home to anyone in love.

Rodgers' chattering guitar opens it in style. Already there with him is Sammy Figueroa, whose congas are such an indelible part of the song. The warm, sunny tones of the music come in large part from Rodgers and the strings. It's a glorious combination, with Edwards' bass swinging somewhere between the two. Kathy's phrasing and delivery are exquisite.

There is a bridge at 2:33 that starts instrumentally with the strings and Rodgers playing the twin melody lines before Kathy comes back in – 'I'm in love again, and it feels so, so good'. We then head into a wave of choruses to the fade out, with Kathy ad-libbing over the top. Overall, this is a marvellous song that leaves you smiling and is a perfect set-up for what follows next.

A stunning 6:36 remix by Dimitri from Paris is in the *Savoir Faire* box set.

'We Are Family'

It's one of those songs where the impact has been reduced by saturation over the years. Its anthemic declaration has even suited many ad campaigns, but if you can clear your mind, it still has a devastating, unstoppable effect. The better-known single edit is only part of the charm. You need to hear the full-length, scintillating album version where the band and Kathy really take off. Joni told Alex Petridis of *The Guardian* in April 2012 that recording the song 'was like a one-take party – we were just dancing and playing around and hanging out in the studio when we did it.' That party atmosphere comes across even before the vocals come in. The instrumental intro 'set-up' is terrific. Allowing time for people to reach the dancefloor, the sisters then hit the first line of the song, which, of course, is the chorus!

Kathy Sledge gives the performance of a lifetime, allegedly recorded in one take. She sings the verses alone, apart from a few backing vocal enhancements, but the choruses are the sisters plus the Chic choir all in unison, apart from 'Get up everybody sing', which is in harmony.

Musically, it is a bubbly, relentless concoction comprised of peaks and even bigger peaks. Everywhere you turn your ears, there is some spectacular musicianship going on. Arguably, the biggest and best is Bernard Edwards, whose bass playing is a revelation – funky and melodic. Kathy's exhortation – 'Come on Bernard' – at 7:48 is an ad-libbed joyous high-point, followed by another one – 'play your funky bass boy' – at 7:55. It gives the song the feel of a live performance. Edwards is just on fire and Kathy *knows* it! She is well in the zone herself, too, now urging on Thompson to 'come on Tony'. Kathy is rightly proud of this section of the song, enthusing to *Popmatters* that 'Having my sisters with me cheering me on, plus Luther (Vandross) and Alfa (Anderson) on background, and Bernard playing that funky bass, I easily got caught up and captured by the music. I'm most proud of that performance.' It was the second single from the album, hitting number eight in Britain and the dizzy heights of number two in America. In 1984, following the success of the remix of 'Lost In Music' by Rodgers, Edwards was at the desk for a remix of this song. It's brighter than the original mix and the snare sound is reverberated and more prominent on the drum track. It got to number 33 in Britain.

'Easier To Love'

One of the lesser tracks on the album, Joni takes lead vocals and does a good job on what is a hidden gem of a song. It's very understated, but the string arrangement is so sensitive and beautiful. It's a perfect gossamer base for Joni's vocals. If you were to put together a compilation of Chic ballads, this would make a very welcome inclusion.

'You're A Friend To Me'

Debbie gets her only lead vocal on this one. In spite of a honey-toned, wandering bass part from Edwards, this is quite a low-key song. Debbie reigns in the vocals, not going for power, and this gives the song a restrained feel that seems at odds with the intensity of the lyrics: a love letter to a lover who is also a friend. There are good aspects to it – Edwards mostly – including a sensitive piano accompaniment and a strong strings arrangement, but there is a sense that the album is cooling off, like a party closing down around you.

'One More Time'

Kim takes lead vocals for this overlooked album closer. Things brighten up, somewhat surprisingly, almost as though the album has been given a shot of adrenaline. It's breezy and light and we even get a guitar solo of sorts from Rodgers. It's one of those sharp, precise, but also melodic pieces he is so good at. This is still an average B-side song at best and is definitely not in the same league as the best the album has to offer. Kim Sledge does give it her all, so credit to her for that.

Their first project for 1979 was originally set to be another outside production. Edwards told the *New Musical Express* in January 1979 that 'next month, we go in with Aretha Franklin.' The *365 Days Of Aretha Franklin* website reported that Rodgers sat at the piano as Aretha sang him 'Only Star'. Rodgers turned down the project, saying he didn't want to be known as 'the guy who wrote Aretha Franklin's disco hit.' He clarified to *Interview* in 2013: 'When Aretha Franklin wanted me to do a disco record for her, I went, 'Huh? Are you kidding me? I know how to write a hit record for you without it being a disco record. You're Aretha Franklin; you don't have to worry about disco." So, no Chic involvement on what was to be her *La Diva* album.

Chic toured Europe in 1979, starting off in Brussels on 4 January and finishing on 20 January back in Brussels, having visited England, Spain, France and Italy in between. Andy Schwartz joined Ray Jones on keyboards. He told David Nathan of *Classic Soul* in 1979:

> I was on the first album, but I didn't do the first tour. Then, after we recorded the second album, I decided it might be fun to go out there for the second tour. Sure, it's taken a minute to adjust, but I've gotten used to it now. And, really, it's like working with a family unit. There's a lot of mutual respect between everyone and that makes working a really enjoyable experience.

Part of the buzz on the tour was, said Anderson in the same interview, down to the singles' success: 'Now that we've got a couple of hits under our belt, it's that much more exciting to come out onstage to roars of approval.' There had been key personnel added, initially just for the tour, on backing vocals. The incoming Alfonso 'Fonzi' Thornton explained to the *PopMatters* website on 11 December 2020 how it came about:

> I was seeing (Alfa) all the time and she said to me, 'Bernard wants to call you because we need to add singers to supplement what Luci and I are doing. They want our live vocals to have the power and soul of the records.' So, Bernard called me and he said, 'Come down and sing with us because we want to try some different things; we have some new ideas.' I called Michelle on the phone. I said, 'Come over here tonight. Let's learn every song they got.' Through years of singing together, Michelle and I blended well, developed similar inflections and dynamics and looked great together. We learned maybe ten of the songs and went down two days later and sang at the audition. 'Nard and Nile said, 'Yeah man, this is cool. Let's go.' We did maybe two weeks of gigs and then they said, 'We're going to go in the studio next week. We want you to sing.

Chic were off the road for most of February to April 1979, which is likely when most of the recording for *Risqué* was completed. They were then back on the road solidly, from May to 1 September, covering the US. One person who saw them live in this era was future Chic saxophonist Bill Holloman. He recalls: 'I was at college in Cincinnati and I saw them at the Ohio Valley Kool Jazz Festival at the Riverfront Stadium in Cincinnati (21 July 1979), sponsored by Kool cigarettes. It wasn't really jazz at all; it was disco black acts. The music was great and Chic were on it with the strings and everything.' Following a much-needed break, Chic returned to Europe for dates running from Amsterdam on 24 September 1979 to Bremen on 18 October. They then returned to America for a run of dates in Los Angeles.

Risqué (Chic) (1979)

Personnel:
Nile Rodgers: guitar, backing vocals
Bernard Edwards: bass, lead vocals on 'My Feet Keep Dancing', backing vocals
Tony Thompson: drums, percussion
Alfa Anderson: lead vocals on 'Good Times', 'My Forbidden Lover', 'Will You Cry' and 'What About Me', backing vocals
Luci Martin: lead vocals on 'Good Times', 'My Feet Keep Dancing', 'My Forbidden Lover' and 'Can't Stand To Love You', backing vocals
Fonzi Thornton lead vocals on 'Good Times' and 'My Forbidden Lover', backing vocals
Michelle Cobbs, Ullanda McCullough: harmony and backing vocals
Sammy Figueroa: percussion
Ray Jones, Rob Sabino, Andy Schwartz: keyboards, piano, clavinet
Cheryl Hong, Karen Milne, Valerie Haywood, Karen Karlsrud: the Chic strings
Gene Orloff: concertmaster
Jon Faddis, Ellen Seeling: trumpet
Jean Fineberg, Alex Foster: saxophone
Barry Rogers: trombone
Fayard Nicholas, Eugene Jackson, Sammy Warren: tap-dance on 'My Feet Keep Dancing'
Produced and arranged by Bernard Edwards & Nile Rodgers at Power Station, New York, Electric Lady (New York) and Kendun Recorders (Burbank), between November 1978 and February 1979
Release date: 30 July 1979
Label: Atlantic
Highest chart places: UK: 29, US: 5
Running time: 36:46
All songs by Edwards and Rodgers.

There are musical changes for this album, notably more keyboards and the strings boosted in the mix. Karen Karlsrud expanded the strings to a quartet for this album only. Vocally, there were bigger changes with the arrival of Michelle Cobbs, Fonzi Thornton and Ullanda McCullough on backing and harmony vocals. The album was recorded and mixed in eight weeks. Chic worked mostly in Studio A at Power Station, but the strings were recorded at Electric Lady: 11 violins, four violas and two cellos. Gene Orloff arranged and conducted those sessions. The brass had already been recorded back at the *C'est Chic*/*We Are Family* sessions. Jean Fineberg says that 'we didn't know until many years later about *Risqué* and that we were on it.' As a sign of the band's growing success, they had to snatch time to finish the lead vocals while back out on tour!

The song selection is as strong as *C'est Chic*. Anderson enthused to *RnB Junkie* in December 2018:

> Everything about *Risqué* – the music, the lyrics, the arrangements, the vocals – makes it one of my favourite Chic albums. We were really in the zone vocally. Fonzi Thornton, Michelle Cobbs, Luci Martin and I perfected the Chic vocal style on 'Good Times' and 'My Forbidden Lover'. The phrasing of those syncopated rhythms worked so well with the music. Above all, we had fun and you can hear that. 'A Warm Summer Night' was sensuous. The strings and the tap dancing on 'My Feet Keep Dancing' were cutting edge. The ballads suited Luci and me perfectly. And oh, that cover!

Yes, that wonderful cover! Looking expensive and stylish, it was designed by Carin Goldberg and photographed by Ken Ambrose. Edwards, in *Blues And Soul* in 1979, explained: 'We decided we'd do something with a theme that tied into some of the tunes, like 'What About Me?', 'My Forbidden Lover' and 'Can't Stand To Love You'. So, there's a whole mini-story linking the songs and the cover. We were thinking about all those old mystery movies and the Agatha Christie books.'

What we get is a murder mystery evolving over the front, back and inside sleeves. The front cover is the final reveal of the three as Edwards lies slumped over his piano, a knife wedged into his back. Looking on are Rodgers (the house guest) with coat and hat on, ready to leave, Thompson (the butler), Anderson (Edwards' wife) and Martin (the maid). But who was the culprit? The rear cover shows Edwards alone at his piano, but the inside album sleeve captures the five before the knife plunged. Edwards is at the piano with Thompson looking on, but Rodgers is busy on the sofa to the rear, entertaining both Anderson and Martin! You have to conclude that he is the killer!

Unfortunately, the same month that the record was released saw the peak of a backlash against disco music. On 12 July 1979, thousands of disco records were blown up at Comiskey Park in Chicago during the break in the match between the White Sox and the Detroit Tigers. Chic were derided (unfairly) in some sections of the media as a disco act. Edwards saw the inherent problem for Chic, telling *Billboard*'s Paul Grein on 17 December 1979 that 'the public put you in a category and decide that you're a disco group, so obviously if disco dies, you have to be concerned.'

The lead-off single was initially intended to be 'My Feet Keep Dancing'. That could have worked, but wisely, Rodgers and Edwards went for 'Good Times'. The attention and sales that this received as it climbed to number one in America ensured the album sold in huge numbers. For me, it's Chic's joint best album, a twin peak with C'est Chic. The cream of Chic's best work – both singles and album tracks are featured on this pair. There are great songs throughout their catalogue, but the consistency throughout these two albums sets them apart.

'Good Times'

An absolute classic and another candidate for their best song. This was the first single from the album and it reached number one in August 1979 in

America. In Britain, it reached number five. As usual, it's the album version I am referencing because it's twice as long as the single!

It's not as overtly euphoric a song as it might seem to be on casual listening, as the lyrics reveal on closer scrutiny. 'That was probably our most ironic composition to date', commented Rodgers in the *Very Best Of Chic* notes. 'As soon as the party in the disco is over, you go back to your humdrum life.' He explained in more detail to *EMPSFM* in June 2000:

> Bernard and I thought about the one time in American musical history when black people were proud, and that was in the era of the big bands. Even though Count Basie and those guys couldn't stay in the hotel, they made their presence felt.
>
> So when we wrote 'Good Times', we went back to the Great Depression. And we went to Al Jolson: 'The stars are going to twinkle and shine, this evening about a quarter to nine'. That's how we started, We didn't look at Al Jolson as being racist. We looked at him as saying, 'This is the music of these people – you'll accept me as a white person putting on this makeup and singing it, but if (a black guy) comes up on stage, you'd boo.'
>
> We went back (also) to 'Happy Days' (by Milton Ager from the 1930s). I mean, this was all seriously thought-out stuff. This was protest shrouded in double-entendre, all of this stuff that had, as Bernard and I used to call it, DHM: deep hidden meaning.

Indeed, the chorus comes over as a mantra – an affirmation or determination to overcome challenging circumstances. The verses are equally positive 'messages' that come over like a series of advertising slogans – for example, 'We want the best, we won't settle for less'.

It was the first track recorded for the album. Rodgers commented on the intro to John Wilson for BBC Radio 4's *Front Row* in 2005:

> It's a gigantic glissando starting at the lower portion of the keyboard and going as far as you can in that couple of seconds. And then we have the women's bathroom at the Power Station as the big echo chamber. We fed the signal into the ladies' bathroom. It was very reflective in there. It's all tiles and stuff like that, so it makes this swirly sound that's bouncing back and forth. It's a subtle technique that winds up becoming this grand, big statement.

It instantly affects me as much as it did on my first hearing. Michelle Cobbs first heard it before there were any vocals. She told *Rolling Stone* in March 2021 that they (the vocalists) knew right away it was a great song: 'When the bassline was formed and the whole beat of the song was there, we just felt that it was going to be a hit. Nile and Bernard know what they are doing. The simplicity of it created the hit. The vocals were very short, simple and exact.'

As well as Cobbs, the lead vocal powerhouse features Anderson, Martin, Thornton and McCullough. It's a vocal tour-de-force.

Thornton recalled to *PopMatters* on 11 December 2020 how the vocals were recorded:

> Bernard said, 'Fonz, go stand in front of the mic.' He had me sing 'Good times, these are the good times'. In fact, the male voice you hear prominently on the line 'Leave your cares behind' is me doing a harmony step out. Bernard said, 'Just double it. Do it again.' I'd sung maybe four tracks and then he brought in Michelle, Alfa and Ullanda. They sang along with me and created the group sound for the choruses.

The reflective tone in the vocals and a sense of wistful longing are uncannily mirrored in the music. Edwards' bass anchors it from the start and the sheer melodic power of his riff never lets up. Rodgers recalled to Paul Lester for *The Guardian* in 2014: 'It was funny the way we discovered that walking bassline; it was a total accident. Bernard started playing something and I screamed, 'Walk!' And he did and that was 'Good Times'. Sammy Figueroa adds, 'That groove with Bernard was just beautiful. I was really proud of what I did there.' It seems only right that the breakdown section, from 3:11, is almost, in effect, a bass solo from the man. 'Good Times' is very much Edwards' song, with Rodgers' parts serving the rhythm and never distracting from that central core bass. Other than the hand claps and Thompson's subtle cymbals, it's Edwards who we get right down to alone on the breakdown. His time in the spotlight for some deep and funky riffing is superb. It's one of the greatest spots in Chic's back catalogue. Ray Jones' Fender Rhodes finally starts to bring things back. It's Rob Sabino who plays the piano parts on the song, most noticeably in the verses.

Praise, too, for other key aspects of the music. The strings are just sensational, with a slashing four-note string riff alternating on the verses. They also stab away and punctuate the choruses with equal drama. Finally, there are the metronomic unison hand claps, which were actually created with a Roland drum machine.

'Good Times' proved to be an inspirational and influential song for other artists. The groove on the bassline turned up, recognisably, in the burgeoning hip-hop scene as The Sugarhill Gang sampled it for 'Rapper's Delight', released in September 1979. Then there was Queen's John Deacon. His subsequent composition, 'Another One Bites The Dust' (1980), also seemed to show his 'admiration' for the bass riff. Jonathan Ross pointedly asked Rodgers and Edwards about this in 1992 on his UK chat show. Edwards explained that 'John was in the studio when we were recording the song and obviously he liked the groove.' Rogers jumped in, adding that the riff was 'Just sort of in the style, it wasn't the actual riff.' Edwards then added that they 'took it as a compliment.'

At the time of writing, 'Good Times' has been sampled in 243 songs! Joni, Debbie and Kim Sledge (as Sister Sledge) recorded a weak cover of it in 1992 for their *And Now Sledge Again* album.

'A Warm Summer Night'

This track has a beautiful, languid, summery feel. Anderson's vocals are airy and light, with some sweet harmonies from Martin. One word proved tricky for Anderson, as she recalled to Christian Wikane for *Pop Matters* in December 2018: 'When we did 'A Warm Summer Night', there's 'Te quiero'. When I first looked at it, I said, 'Tay key-err-o!' because I didn't know any Spanish. They laughed and laughed. That's why Luci ended up speaking that part because I was going to enunciate every little consonant and make sure that all the vowels were there.'

Rodgers complements the vocals with delicate picking, while the rhythm section are understated, with Edwards playing a melodic bassline. The bridge (at 3:18) is a particular delight, with a lyrical piano as the lead instrument. However, at just over six minutes, the track is overlong and could have done with losing a minute or so.

'My Feet Keep Dancing'

The band's third single from the album pretty much said they were on the wane as a chart act in America, stalling at number 101. In Britain, it reached a reasonable number 21.

It follows the tradition of their previous dance-inspired songs but has the added value of a tap-dance solo from Fayard Nicholas of the esteemed Nicholas Brothers. Rodgers recalled in the *Very Best Of Chic* notes in 2000: 'We were paying homage to the pioneers who came before us. That's why we flew out to California and brought in Fayard Nicholas. He listened to our music, dug it and started tap-dancing to it. We thought that was amazing.' Note that the credits also include Eugene Jackson (of Our Gang) and Sammy Warren as contributing.

The hypnotic feel of the song is there right from the intro. The melodic factor at the heart of all this is the keyboards, which pop out at the end of each vocal line. Martin and Edwards duet in the verses, their voices blending well, as they outline the things they need/long to do in the first verse, 'Fly into space, or maybe save the human race' being the biggest stretch. But none of these things are possible when your feet keep dancing! Keep an ear on Edwards in the verse; his bass riff sounds similar to the formidable one on 'Everybody Dance' and it's as potent here, too. After two times round on the chorus, the hypnotic repeated title starts to wear thin. Even the Chic choir can't do much with it. Verse two is interesting as there's a sense of acceptance and resolution, a way out as Martin and Edwards realise 'I had to be what I was meant to be'. It sets up a two-minute-long finale of the chorus repeated ad infinitum.

'My Forbidden Lover'

The second single from the album, this is sung from the perspective of a woman who has a 'forbidden lover'. She can't resist him but is nonetheless fully aware of his shortcomings. In the end, it appears she does come to terms with her situation because there's a delightful playfulness in the melody and rhythm that suggests things are going pretty well. This is mirrored in the warm and confidential nature of the vocals, especially in the verses, even as Anderson and Martin outline 'his' faults. It all makes for a light, poppy song, albeit somewhat lacking in substance. Edwards' supple bass holds it all together, while Rodgers plays hard (to get)!

An extended remix (6:26) was featured on the 12" single and is in the *Savoir Faire* box set. This features a longer intro and has the clavinet mixed up much higher, so it's one of the dominant instruments. It also features an instrumental break at 4:34, which adds a welcome variation with Fender Rhodes, clavinet and Rodgers vying for your attention. Dimitri From Paris also came up with a superb remix, which showcases the piano and clavinet even more. It also has a lovely, slow intro that sets the song up superbly.

'Can't Stand To Love You'

Martin takes the verses, joined by Anderson and the others for the choruses. In fact, the verses would have worked better as a duet – it does sound like they are supposed to be that way because Martin sings call-and-response to herself, altering her delivery for the 'other person'! Rodgers' opening guitar hints at a tougher sound to come, but instead, it falls back on a jerky, dynamic rhythm. It's an average song, but it could have been better with more drama in the arrangement. It's just too jaunty for the lyrics, which allude to domestic disharmony and even marital violence: 'The way that you treated me, You'd think I were into S&M!'

'Will You Cry (When You Hear This Song)'

This one has plenty of emotional soul-baring as befits the latest in a line of gorgeous ballads. Anderson turns in a stellar vocal performance in the verses, her intonation and delivery being superb. As usual, it's everyone to the microphone for the chorus, but surprisingly, it lacks the strength of the verses a little. There's a nice instrumental break at 2:00, with a duet between the strings and Rodgers. The arrangement is excellent throughout, and I especially love the cool-down from 3:48 in the outro. It's just a sweet little coda that features piano tinkles over the strings. This is an excellent song, in spite of the chorus just missing the mark.

A 7:50 outtake version closes the *Savoir Faire* box set. The bulk of this is the band attempting a run-through of the song, broken up by much hilarity. It's a 'play once' track, which Rodgers likely included to represent the fun they had working together in the studio. Thompson reminisced to *One Two*

Testing in 1985: 'We used to have so much fun in the studio, a ball. If people knew how much laughing was going on behind those tracks.'

'What About Me?'

'That was a song that Bernard basically wrote and I helped with it', recalled Rodgers in the *Very Best Of Chic* notes in 2000. It's a strident finish to the album, the clavinet being a welcome addition to the rhythm track, adding extra power. Anderson sings the verses with Martin and the backing vocalists come in for the choruses.

What it lacks is more subtlety in the arrangement. The strings are great and provide contrast to the main melody, but much more from Rodgers would have helped. He is a little too low in the mix on the rhythm track. The generally understated mix doesn't do this track any favours.

A 2:47 instrumental outtake was included in the *Savoir Faire* set and illustrates what could have been achieved on the album track. It is immediately more interesting because Rodgers is right up in the mix. With the focus on his guitar rhythm leading strongly from the front, it sounds punchier. Add some vocals to this outtake and it would have been terrific.

Prior to the band's UK dates in late 1979, Rodgers outlined their live plans to David Nathan of *Classic Soul* in October 1979:

> We're concerned about projecting more entertainment value in our show. That will mean more props, lighting, special effects and so on because we really want to dramatise the songs more. Not just come out there and do the hits because people expect you to just do that in a standard way. There's going to be more playing and singing, more dancing and more hard work! That should begin at the beginning of next year, although we'll be trying some things on our European tour.

Along with the regular five, the band consisted of Thornton and Cobbs on backing vocals, Ray Jones and Andy Schwartz on keyboards, plus the Chic strings. Setlists are rare to find for Chic but at Hammersmith Odeon on 9 October, they played 'Chic Cheer', 'I Want Your Love', 'My Forbidden Lover', 'He's The Greatest Dancer', 'Lost In Music', 'We Are Family', 'At Last I Am Free', 'Dance, Dance, Dance', 'Le Freak', 'Everybody Dance', 'My Feet Keep Dancing' and 'Good Times'. There is some footage from Hammersmith online. A review on *Chictribute* by Derek Bussen of a show at Michigan State Fair on 28 August says they played 'A Warm Summer Night', so perhaps this, too, was in the setlist at Hammersmith.

Les Plus Grands Succes De Chic (Chic) (Atlantic, 1979)

This was rushed out in December 1979 and surely set some kind of record for the release of a greatest-hits album. The cover image is one of the best of the band and captures the joy and spirit of the music. The tracklist is the singles to date, which means that some key album-only tracks ('At Last I Am Free', for example) are not included. Even concentrating on the singles presented problems. America got 'Chic Cheer', while everywhere else got 'My Forbidden Lover'. In fact, you would want both on the album, but the running time was an issue.

Of the remaining tracks, only 'Everybody Dance' and 'Good Times' were featured in their preferred 12" mixes and three ('Dance, Dance, Dance', 'Le Freak' and 'I Want Your Love') are the 7" single edits. So, it makes for a package that should have been longer and better, but that would have meant a double album and there were only three albums to pick from in the first place!

Love Somebody Today (Sister Sledge) (1980)

Personnel:
Debbie Sledge, Joni Sledge, Kathy Sledge, Kim Sledge: lead vocals (see songs for credits)
Nile Rodgers: guitar
Bernard Edwards: bass
Tony Thompson: drums
Sammy Figueroa: percussion
Ray Jones, Andy Schwartz (Edwards): keyboards, Fender Rhodes, piano
Rob Sabino: piano, clavinet
Cheryl Hong, Karen Milne, Marianne Carroll: the Chic strings
Gene Orloff: concert master
Alfa Anderson, Michelle Cobbs, Luci Martin, Fonzi Thornton: backing vocals on 'Got To Love Somebody'
Jean Fineberg, Ellen Seeling, Jon Faddis, Alex Foster, Bob Milliken, Meco: brass on 'Got To Love Somebody'
Eddie Daniels: saxophone solo on 'Gotta Love Somebody' and 'Reach Your Peak'
Produced and arranged by Bernard Edwards and Nile Rodgers, between November 1979 and February 1980
Release date: 16 March 1980
Label: Cotillion
Highest chart places: UK: did not chart, US: 31
Running time: 38:44
All songs by Edwards and Rodgers.

The follow-up to *We Are Family* sees the sisters stamping more of their own style. As part of that, the Organisation's backing singers are not present on any track other than the near title song. The difference in the sound, however, is enormous without them. The album lacks the same cohesion and impact as its predecessor, and the cover looks cheaper, too. The expensive-looking *We Are Family* cover has been succeeded by a very average close-up of the sisters.

Jean Fineberg isn't credited on the sleeve but is featured. She says: 'I would have played on it. Ellen (Seeling) never played on anything that I didn't play on.' One of the featured players is Eddie Daniels, who recalls, 'I was told to bring alto and tenor saxophones with me. I am the solo sax on 'Gotta Love Somebody' and 'Reach Your Peak'.' Surprisingly, Daniels was there to record the overdubs on his own: 'Bernard and Nile were not there. As far as I remember, it was only me and the engineer. I made up the solos on the spot and played through everything for as long as he let me, so they could use it in more places. I am not sure if there was even a chart! I just dove in!'

Little else is known about the sessions, possibly because the album didn't have the same impact as *We Are Family*. Although the album did reasonably well in America, it was a commercial flop in Britain. There was little interest in the singles either, with only 'Got To Love Somebody' making much of a splash, reaching number 64 in America and number 34 in Britain.

'Got To Love Somebody'

This is the only track to feature the brass section, which was used on *C'est Chic* and *We Are Family.* From Seeling and Fienberg's recollections, this means this track is effectively an outtake from *We Are Family.* Their inclusion, plus the strings and the backing choir, make this the biggest Chic-sounding track on the album, and also the best.

Kathy Sledge sings with a similarly raw, impassioned voice to the one she used on *We Are Family*'s title track. The skipping rhythm makes great use of Figueroa's shakers, and the brass adds extra presence to the chorus. Meanwhile, the Rodgers/Edwards/Thompson rhythm section keep it tight and focused. Eddie Daniels' sax solo (which comes in at 2:35) makes for a different style bridge to the Chic norm, and there is no breakdown on this song! It's a breezy solo which suits the airy feel of the tune. It's a long song (well over six minutes) and the second half (after the sax solo) is mostly Kathy scatting over the rhythm with Daniels coming back in as a wild card soloist behind her. Her extra strength on the words 'somebody today' at 5:00 is one of the high points of the song. Daniels pops up again on the extended outro, which sees Kathy mixed down to give him space. Somehow, even though the lyrics and Kathy's delivery are full of forlorn desperation, this still manages to be an uplifting song.

Dimitri From Paris's excellent remix is 33 seconds longer and opens up the sound spectrum, with the benefit of extra sax too. The core of the melody was used for the 2015 Chic reboot single 'I'll Be There'.

'You Fooled Around'

Kathy takes the lead again on this silky pop song. It's much in the vein of 'He's The Greatest Dancer', with a similar warm glow. That 'glow' is a little odd given that the lyrics reveal how and why the relationship hit the rocks. Despite the inconsistency, you can't fault the glossy perfection on display. The plucked (heart) strings in the more rhythmic verses are terrific and really enhance the song. By contrast, the legato strings have an airy feel to them in the choruses. Figueroa uses some form of bells, which don't quite fit for me – you can't help but think of a sleigh coming along. This is still a classy song, in large part due to the vocals singing against the wonderful strings.

'I'm A Good Girl'

There is some great piano by Sabino here. The song could easily have worked as a ballad with little more than the piano backing Joni Sledge. She is, in fact, the only vocalist on the track, which emphasises the personal nature of the lyrics.

There are two aspects of the song I struggle with. There are parts, such as at 0:56, where it speeds up, in which Joni's delivery fails to adapt to the musical changes. Then, there's the chorus which almost interrupts to the verses rather than being its own euphoric section. It just never feels quite right. That being said, it's pleasant enough and the bare bones of Joni and the piano is excellent.

'Easy Street'

This is Kim's only solo lead vocal. She is probably the weakest of the four sisters vocally, as exemplified by the opportunities she gets to sing lead on their albums. Sadly, this one definitely suffers because her vocals just aren't strong enough. When the backing vocals come in for the choruses, it's instantly a better sound. That being said, it's an average song at best in the first place, with Kim finding the place where 'the grass is greener' – her happy home on Easy Street. The contentment that successfully comes across permeates the backing track, too, with only Edwards' bass catching your ear.

'Reach Your Peak'

Joni gets to sing this one with a lyric that naughtily sees her 'reaching her peak' – simulating orgasm. The Chic strings take centre stage in the bridge at 2:04, accompanied by Eddie Daniels again on sax, who finishes off with a customary fine jazzy solo as we head for that peak. The music then drops down at 3:08 behind the sisters singing lead vocals in unison and adding harmony backing vocals. It's a terrific section of the song, showing off their vocal power and talents. Joni finally reaches that peak with a self-conscious laugh to herself afterwards.

There was a 12" released, which is 5:25 – not much longer than the album version. You do, however, hear Daniels get to start another solo, which is cut off. It was the second single and got to number 101 in America.

'Pretty Baby'

All four sisters sing lead in unison on this one. They rarely seem to do this, and when they do, they sound amazing. Behind them, the backing track powers along on a driving three-note riff from Rodgers, which is the pulse of this lyrically dark song. Although this is a basic backing track, the counterpoint of the vocals against Rodgers makes this a track to come back to.

'How To Love'

Kathy is back on lead vocals for this one. It isn't dissimilar to 'I'm A Good Girl', with its relaxed, conversational tone. The string arrangement is especially gorgeous, soaring around Andy Schwartz's beautifully performed piano. Kathy gives a typically assured performance on this lovely, shimmering track.

'Let's Go On Vacation'

A happy tune to finish the album, but this doesn't crown things off well. Debbie takes the verses with her sisters coming in for the chorus. It's cheerful and breezy, but it needed much more fun and bounce. They don't really sell the song vocally – the chorus, in particular, falls short on enthusiasm or excitement about the vacation. The big problem, though, is that the song is average. Aside from the vocals, even the backing track is lacklustre, apart from an excellent jazzy keyboard part.

It was the third single from the album, but didn't trouble any charts. Clearly, Rodgers and Edwards liked it a lot as they featured it on the *Soup For One* soundtrack.

Diana (Diana Ross) (1980)

Personnel:
Diana Ross: lead vocals
Nile Rodgers: guitar
Bernard Edwards: bass
Tony Thompson: drums, percussion
Fonzi Thornton, Alfa Anderson, Luci Martin, Michelle Cobbs: harmony and backing vocals
Ray Jones: keyboards, Fender Rhodes
Andy Schwartz: piano
Cheryl Hong, Karen Milne, Valerie Haywood: the Chic strings
Gene Orloff: concert master
Meco Monardo: trombone
Bob Milliken: trumpet
Eddie Daniels: saxophone
Produced and arranged by Bernard Edwards and Nile Rodgers, between November 1979 and February 1980
Release date: 22 May 1980
Label: Tamla Motown
Highest chart places: UK: 12, US: 2
Running time: 34:17

This was the biggest project yet for Rodgers and Edwards, working with an established star with a significant back catalogue and sales to match. Expectations were high, but Rodgers pinpointed a key intention to *Jet Magazine* in 1979. 'When we met Diana', he recalled, 'she said she wanted to get back to having fun.' The big idea from Tamla was to break Diana out into a wider market and eclipse previous sales figures. Charged with achieving that goal was President of Motown Productions Suzanne de Passe (second only to label founder Berry Gordy in terms of authority). De Passe was a fan of the Chic Organisation and she saw them as being the people to deliver on Tamla's ambitions. It was a big decision, but it was one that paid off, although not without angst.

The song that became central to the concept was 'I'm Coming Out'. Rodgers explained how that came about to *Interview* in 2013:

> One night when I was out club-hopping, I stopped into the Gilded Grape on Eighth Avenue in the Theater District. While I was there, I went to the bathroom and on either side of me were these Diana Ross impersonators, which is what gave me the idea for 'I'm Coming Out'. The double entendre was that we knew that Diana Ross was planning a big move – maybe she wasn't going to leave Motown, but she certainly was going to ask for a portion of the company. We knew she had a master plan. So we wrote the song about it – from her point of view. But from my point of view, it was about the gay community.

The gestation of the songs came from conversations Rodgers and Edwards had with Ross about the direction she wanted to go in for the album, and aspects of her life at the time. Lyrically, the songs are often their comments on her thoughts, giving the album a very personal perspective. Rodgers revealed in *Le Freak*: 'We included excessively polysyllabic words like 'instinctively' and 'respectfully' in the lyrics because we wanted to utilise Diana's sophistication to achieve a higher level of musicality.' Both of these examples can be heard on 'Upside Down'.

They started the backing tracks at Power Station in November 1979. The first four worked on were 'I'm Coming Out', 'Give Up', 'Tenderness' and 'Upside Down' (then titled 'The Work Song'). This continued into January 1980. A big difference in the recording process came with recording the vocals. No line-by-line work for Diana Ross. Thornton told *Pop Matters* on 11 December 2020: 'The only songs that I ever heard before we recorded them were the *Diana* songs because I sang the reference vocals.' He also revealed that Alfa Anderson was originally asked to do the reference vocals, but Ross told Rodgers and Edwards, 'I don't want to hear a woman singing these songs. Don't you have a guy that can sing these songs?' One song that didn't make the cut was 'I've Got Protection', which Thornton suspected Ross rejected because of the reference to infection! The album has one major sequencing curiosity in not opening with 'I'm Coming Out'. As the song that is so central to the project, with such a big intro, why wasn't it track one?

When they turned in the final mix, it was met with criticism from Motown. Berry Gordy's observation, recalled Rodgers in *Le Freak,* was that "Upside Down' is not a Diana Ross record and neither is the rest of the album.' Rodgers was stunned; Ross had, all along, insisted, 'you're writing songs for me now', he told *Freeze Frame* in 1981. So he and Edwards were upset at the reaction to their work because, as Rodgers emphasised to Larry Flick at *Billboard* in February 2000, 'When I'm in the studio, I'm trying to make the best record I can. I'm not trying to show how great I am, but how great the artist is.' He further elaborated to *Computer Music* in June 2006: 'To me, the artist always has the final word: it's their picture on the cover of the record.'

That final word likely came from both Ross and the decision makers at Motown. A remix was performed by Ross's regular engineer Ross Terrana. He commented in the deluxe CD booklet on what he felt were the issues with Chic's original mix: 'It had a very nice, clean, rich sound, but I felt a song would come on, and 20 seconds later, it was still there – no peaks and valleys. The dynamics seemed limited.' Most damningly, he concurred: 'It sounded like a Chic album with a Diana Ross voice. It wasn't a Diana Ross album.' In the same booklet, Brian Chin said that, 'crucially, a close mic'd, laid-back set of Ross's lead performances was chosen for the 'official' album, in contrast to her gutsy vocal attack in the original Rodgers/Edwards mixes.' Those close-mic'd vocals were all newly recorded by Ross and completed in April 1980 at Hittsville Studios in Los Angeles. Other than new vocals, Terrana also aimed to 'create the dynamics that seemed missing, so you could feel the emotions change, and hear the subtleties already in the music.'

The greyscale cover image of the album showed a tougher, almost 'street' side to Ross. It's saying this is the 'new me', but for those who might have been unsure by it, there's a more glamorous and inviting image all over the inside of the gatefold sleeve.

Rodgers and Edwards were oblivious to the remix until the album was released. Both men were gutted, probably especially Rodgers, whose guitar is often dialled down on Terrana's mixes. It would be a long wait before their original mix was finally released on the deluxe edition in 2001. Notes on the differences between the two mixes are under each song below. Whichever mix you prefer, the album has a sleek, refined soul/jazz feel to it. It sees the Organisation moving firmly away from disco. Harder edges were to appear on their final two releases of the year.

Despite the mixing issues, Rodgers and Edwards were asked to produce Ross's next album. But that remix, plus possibly some of the teething troubles in recording the album, swayed their response. There was to be no follow-up album.

'Upside Down'

It was the first single and it got to number one in America and number two in the UK. The lyrical inspiration came from Diana's admission in *Le Freak* that her life was at a 'time of major change' and that she was 'looking forward to turning my world around.'

On Chic's original mix, Rodgers told *Sound On Sound* in April 2005: 'I keyed the funky rhythm of the strings. They played it straight; there was no way they could play like that. I'll never forget when we turned that record over to Motown, we asked, 'What happened to those funky strings? I can't believe you guys erased those funky strings!' I can still hear myself: 'What kind of engineers have you got? They couldn't figure that out?'

It's a little different for Chic at this time, missing out on the sparkling keyboard runs and having a sharper staccato chord pattern. The sawing strings contribute to the angular feel on the choruses. The verses are a little more relaxed. Ross sings it well, but there's no sense of her stretching out at any point; it's almost conversational. The best part of the song is the outro section, which starts at 2:40. The backing vocalists step up for the first time and their added weight gives the song more verve. A very good song suddenly turns into something much better. Rodgers, who has been quiet, contributes choppy rhythm guitar, mixed well up from 3:18, which dominates the instrumental section that closes the song.

The original Chic mix doesn't have the punch and impact of Terrana's mix. Everything is more blended together. It's also a softer vocal from Ross, with a slight chorus effect on her voice. A big plus in the Chic mix, however, is the extra string section parts.

'Tenderness'

Rodgers and Edwards were so impressed by Ross's gentle, kindly side that they wrote this song. The verses are strong, with the backing harmonies interacting well with Ross. The chorus, however, is too repetitive, with little to distinguish it.

Terrana tightened the length up. It runs to 3:52, whereas the original Chic mix is 5:10. The Chic mix is fuller and warmer and Ross sounds better for it. The extra minute or so is prime Chic, too – a glorious, grooving, long outro with the strings in full flight over the tight backing track. You can understand Terrana chopping this part because it does showcase Chic more than Ross, but removing it reduced the song's impact

'Friend To Friend'

This ballad was written as a tribute to both Ross and Suzanne de Passe. Stylistically, it's in the vein of the classic Chic ballads. Terrana's mix does have an elegance to it, but it misses the piano, which is a feature of the original Chic mix. There is a Fender Rhodes part on this, but it's mixed too low. The arrangement, as per Terrana's mix, is understated, subtle and quiet. Rodgers contributes a slightly shrill, jazzy solo in the bridge section, and this, too, I think would have been better as a piano solo. Terrana's big decision to turn off the echo effect on Rodgers' guitar was a good one.

The Chic original mix is way better; it's lusher and more rounded. There is a delightful piano part over the intro that adds an extra melodic heart to the song. Ross's voice works better in this environment. Rodgers' rhythm guitar, though, disappoints. It has an irritating echo on it throughout – irritating, that is, until his solo comes in. Here it works much better as a backing track for his solo, which itself sounds all the better for it! So, ideally, they would have had the rhythm echo just on the solo section. The final outro is far more impressive on the Chic mix. You hear Rodgers and the returning piano refrain, whereas Terrana dials it down to just bass and the strings as Ross sings her last words.

It's a draw between the two mixes as to which is best. A composite between the two would be the best version – keeping the piano and losing much of that echoed rhythm guitar.

'I'm Coming Out'

This was the third single from the album and got to number 13 in the UK. This colossal song should have opened the album. That it didn't was presumably because it was felt to be too high risk given the strong message and stylistic change on offer. When a song has this much impact and exuberance, it fully deserved to lead off the album, and its success as a single underlines that.

The two big aspects of the intro are firstly Ross, who sounds like she is coming to terms with her 'situation' – she gets a mix of vulnerability and

Above: Bernard Edwards and Nile Rodgers in the Power Station studio in New York on 29 July 1981. (*Allan Tannenbaum/Getty Images*)

Below: The classic five lineup. From left to right: Luci Martin, Tony Thompson, Alfa Anderson, Bernard Edwards and Nile Rodgers. (*author collection*)

Left: *Chic* (1977). The debut album was an excellent start, featuring two classic songs, but the cover should have had the actual band on it. (*Atlantic*)

Right: *Norma Jean* (1978). The first 'outside' production by Chic was for Norma Jean Wright, who sang on their debut album. It's an essential listen for Chic fans. (*Bearsville*)

Left: *C'est Chic* (1978). The second album by Chic is packed with hits and strong album tracks. Alfa Anderson is joined by Luci Martin for the first time. (*Atlantic*)

Right: 'I Want Your Love' picture sleeve single (1979). One of Chic's very best songs; it reached number four in the UK and number seven in America. (*Atlantic*)

Left: *We Are Family* (1978). Their best outside production was this album for Sister Sledge. It was recorded at the same time as *C'est Chic* and features many great songs. (*Atlantic*)

Right: 'Good Times' picture sleeve single (1979). This is one of the most sampled tunes of all time. It reached number five in the UK and number one in America. Note the misspelt B-side! (*Atlantic*)

Left: Chic on *American Bandstand* in January 1979. Visible behind the front four are Tony Thompson, Michelle Cobbs, Fonzi Thornton and Andy Schwartz. (*author collection*)

Right: Norma Jean Wright. She sang on the debut Chic album and tour. Her wonderful solo album was also a Chic Organisation production. She has worked in recent years again with Luci Martin. (*author collection*)

Below: Sister Sledge watch Edwards and Rodgers at work on their album in Power Station in 1978. (*author collection*)

Right: Rodgers and Edwards onstage in 1979. The two men jointly owned the Chic Organisation company. (*author collection*)

Above: Luci Martin and Alfa Anderson, very much *the* Chic lead vocalists, onstage in 1979. Ray Jones is visible behind them on keyboards. (*author collection*)

Right: Michelle Cobbs and Fonzi Thornton were a key part of the Chic choir. Here they are onstage in 1980. (*author collection*)

Left: The front four were always an eye-catching sight. Martin, Rodgers, Edwards and Anderson vamp it up onstage in 1979. (*author collection*)

Right: The Chic Strings onstage in 1979. From left to right: Valerie Heywood, Cheryl Hong and Karen Milne. (*author collection*)

Left: The fabulous Ray Jones toured with the band and played on most of the albums. He also later worked on a solo project with Norma Jean Wright. (*author collection*)

Right: Tony Thompson, Chic's superb drummer. Among many appearances with other artists, he played with Led Zeppelin at Live Aid. (*author collection*)

Left: Debbie Harry and Nile Rodgers recording her debut solo album *KooKoo* at Power Station in 1981. (*author collection*)

Right: David Bowie, Stevie Ray Vaughan and Nile Rodgers at the launch for *Let's Dance* in 1983. The partnership between the three made the album a huge success. (*author collection*)

Left: *Risque* (1979). Chic's marvellous third album, in a murder/mystery inspired sleeve, is the twin pinnacle of their albums along with *C'est Chic*. (*Atlantic*)

Right: *Les Plus Grands Succes De Chic* (1979). A stunning collection of the singles so far, with an exuberant cover shot that perfectly captures the band's sense of joy and fun. (*Atlantic*)

Left: *Love Somebody Today* (1980). Sister Sledge's follow-up to *We Are Family* isn't as good, but one or two tracks, especially the near title track, are excellent. (*Cotillion*)

Right: *Diana* (1980). Diana Ross's biggest-selling album has some classic songs. The Rodgers and Edwards mix, to their chagrin, was replaced for the original release. (*Motown*)

Left: *King Of The World* (1980). The Sheila & B. Devotion album has some fine songs, including an out-and-out Chic classic in the dance-floor filling 'Spacer'. (*Carrere*)

Right: *Real People* (1980). Chic hit the 1980s with an excellent album that features Rodgers playing some credible rock lead guitar licks for the first time. (*Atlantic*)

Left: *I Love My Lady* (1981). Initially shelved by the label, it finally got released in 2017 and proved to be an excellent amalgam of Chic and Mathis. (*Columbia*)

Right: *KooKoo* (1981). Debbie Harry's debut solo album didn't live up to the expectations of her working with Chic. Neither party is at their best, but the record has its moments. (*Chrysalis*)

Left: *Take It Off* (1981). This brass-heavy Chic album with no Chic Strings sees the guys and girls getting down and funky. (*Atlantic*)

Right: *Soup For One* (1982). The film 'soundtrack' album contains some old tunes and some new ones, of which the very best is Carly Simon's stunning 'Why'. (*Mirage*)

Left: *Tongue In Chic* (1982). Another funk-influenced album and still no Chic Strings. Will the boys ever learn? A fine record, nevertheless. (*Atlantic*)

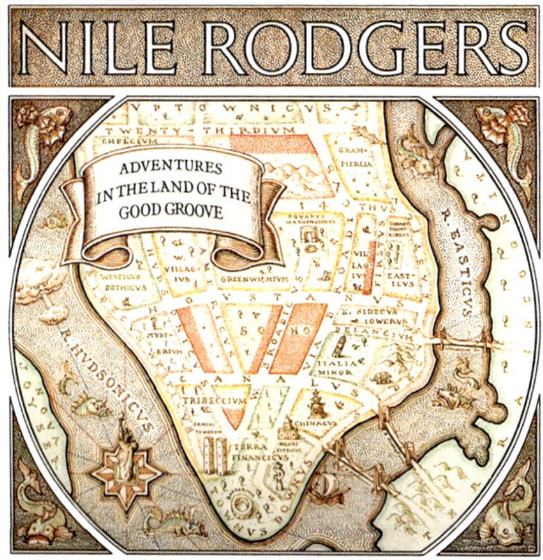

Right: *Adventures In The Land Of The Good Groove* (1983). Rodgers' first solo album features his Chic colleagues. (*Mirage*)

Left: A promotional image of Nile Rodgers in the 1980s. His work with Bowie and Madonna in this decade was his commercial pinnacle. (*author collection*)

Right: Something a bit like this? Bernard Edwards on bass in the control room at Power Station. (*author collection*)

Left: Rodgers and Madonna recording *Like A Virgin* (1984). The picture originally appeared in the September 1984 Japanese edition of *Player* magazine.

Above left: Sylver Logan Sharp, Nile Rodgers and Jessica Wagner. The years with Sharp and Wagner saw Nile Rodgers and Chic establish themselves as a successful live act. (*author collection*)

Above right: Rodgers, in more recent years, in his Le Crib recording studio. (*author collection*)

Above: Nile Rodgers, still leading from the front in the 2020s. (*Rex/Shutterstock*)

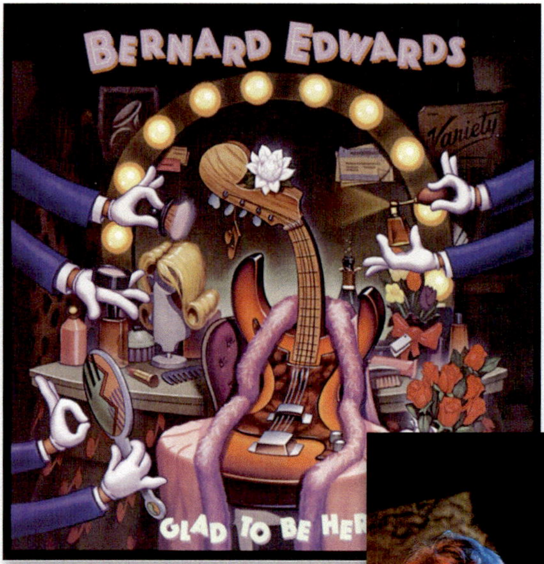

Left: *Glad To Be Here* (1983). Edwards' only solo album features several Chic members. It's a good album, but it doesn't hit the Chic high spots. (*Atlantic*)

Right: *Let's Dance* (1983). Aided by Rodgers and Chic, this is David Bowie's biggest-selling album. The Chicest track is 'Without You', on which Edwards makes his only appearance. (*EMI*)

Left: *Believer* (1983). The final Chic album is a reduced band effort with no brass or strings. It does have some great songs, and Anderson and Martin are in terrific form. (*Atlantic*)

Right: *Like A Virgin* (1984). Madonna's second biggest-selling original album features all of Chic. Perhaps the best listen for Chic fans is the quite sublime 'Shoo-Bee-Doo'. (*WEA*)

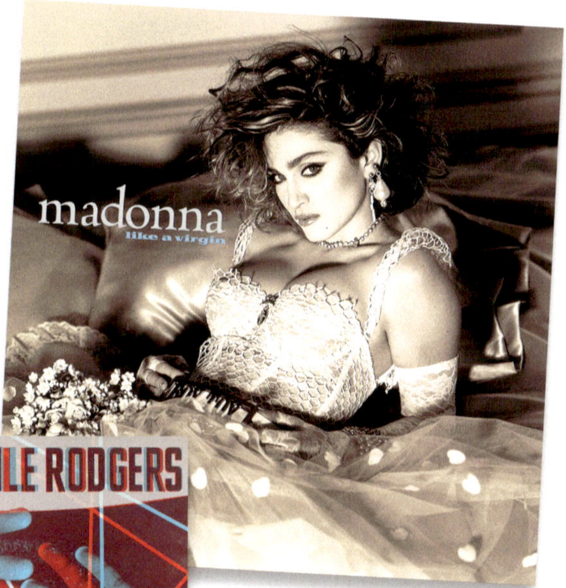

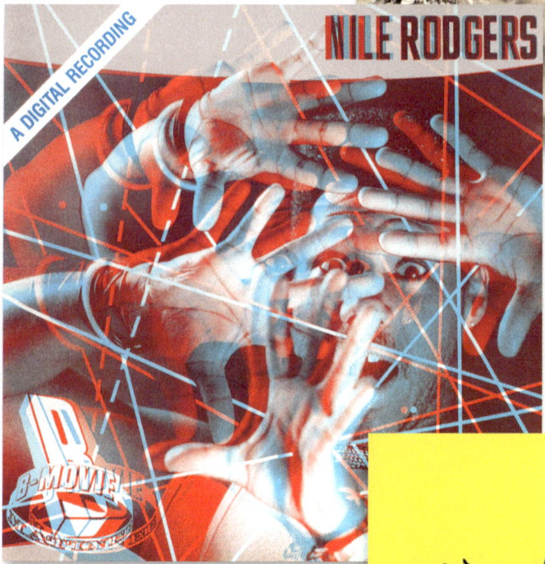

Left: *B-Movie Matinee* (1985). The second solo album from Rodgers displays a more electronic feel than his first, with Rob Sabino on keyboards and a guest appearance from Alfa Anderson. (*Warners*)

Right: *Chic-ism* (1992) The return of Chic. Rodgers and Edwards, with some old friends and some new, get close at times to the glory years. (*Warners*)

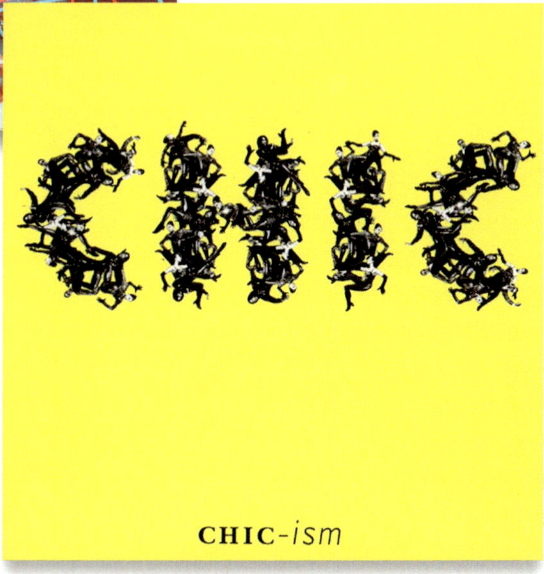

Left: *Chic Freak & More Treats* (1996). This is pretty much a Rodgers project, but also includes Edwards. It's mostly sub-par reworkings of old Chic Organisation tunes. (*Video Arts*)

Right: *Live At The Budokan* (1999). This would have been the new start for Chic, but all that was overshadowed by the death of Edwards after the show. (*Sumthing Else*)

Left: *It's About Time* (2018). After years of tours, Nile Rodgers and Chic finally recorded an album. Sadly, it didn't equal the magnificence of the pre-album single 'I'll Be There'. (*EMI*)

confidence superbly well into her vocals. Then, there's Thompson's monstrously powerful drums, which overshadow the supremely busy work by Rodgers, who is working overtime on rhythm guitar.

Terrana's mix focuses on the dynamics, so the song hits harder and is punchier. One casualty is Rodgers. His primary rhythm part is there, but his secondary guitar, which comes in with a lick at the end of each of Ross's lines in the verses, is faded lower. It's there, but you want to fade it up. The trombone solo lets things down – it just sounds awkward and doesn't have the joy that this song requires. Far better would have been an expressive saxophone solo. Ross's final jubilant 'I'm coming out' at 5:08 is the perfect sign-off.

A so-called 'Instrumental Mix' emerged on YouTube. In spite of it being instrumental, it also shows off the work of the backing vocalists, as they are there singing the choruses. It's also nice because Ray Jones' Fender Rhodes touches 'pop' out of the mix more audibly.

The original Chic mix loses the impact of Ross Terrana's dynamics. It also has a different (even worse) take of the trombone solo. The different vocal track most noticeably varies on Ross's majorly affirmative 'I'm coming out'; on the Chic mix, she sounds unsure of the words, but it suggests a hint of insecurity behind her assertive stance. Chief beneficiary on the Chic mix is Rodgers, whose every note is more audible. The outro gains an extra 30 seconds, which is fine by me because this is such a great song in either mix.

'Have Fun (Again)'

'My new life's going to be fun and adventurous', Diana told Rodgers and Edwards, according to *Le Freak*. Those words prompted a song celebrating her intent. Terrana had trouble with this one. His 5:57 mix is punchier, but Ross's vocal isn't as 'warm' as it is on the Chic original mix. He cut part of the middle section of the song and some of the outro, which means the extended Chic mix goes on until 7:09. It's another of the lesser songs on the album, and that's because Ross doesn't sound like she is giving the song anything special.

The original Chic mix is much better, in part because we get more of the band. Ross's vocal here is more directly suited to the song's theme, as stated earlier, and the mix sounds 'fuller'. The chorus, in particular, is more emphatic. The strings and Rodger are both mixed up higher, which helps fill out the sound. Another key difference is Ross's 'solo' vocal at 2:55, which is stronger and more expressive than on Terrana's mixed new vocal. Likewise, Edwards' bass licks at 3:44 leap out of the speakers at you more. His funky tones are a delight here, and Ross sounds suitably appreciative! Another comparison is the fade-down and fade-up section, which closes the song. It occurs at 4:31 on Terrana's mix and at 5:17 on the Chic mix. Terrana's mix here is flatter and he brings Ross back in much sooner. The Chic mix has a longer jam as it fades back up and they hold back longer on bringing Ross back in.

'My Old Piano'

This was the second single from the album and got to number five in the UK. The baby grand piano in Diana's apartment inspired Rodgers and Edwards to write it. It's the best performance on the album from the band, with some dazzling interplay. It's also the song that sees the most variation between the two mixes, and the winner here is the Chic mix.

Terrana opens his mix with an instrumental section with 'popping' percussive noises. From there, it's into the effervescent chorus, which suits Ross's voice. Both Rodgers and Edwards are outstanding, but it's Edwards' 'elastic' bass playing that grabs your attention at the heart of the mix. All this would be more than enough to keep anyone happy – until you hear the Chic mix.

The Chic mix is a minute longer and is vastly superior, albeit it sounds much 'flatter' with less dynamics than Terrana's mix. But the benefits otherwise are immense. It's straight into the chorus in the intro for a start. Then Rodgers is turned right up and his riff stands out more, wrapping around Ross on the verses. We also get a marvellous extended guitar solo of sorts from Rodgers dovetailing with equally vibrant solo piano from Andy Schwartz. Both men come in at 2:50 and start by playing melodies around Ross's vocals before she drops out, leaving the two men to duet together, trading lines.

In an ideal world, there would be a Terrana remix of the Chic mix that doesn't lose the extended guitar/piano solo.

'Now That You're Gone'

This is a lovely, yearning ballad with an almost reggae feel in the rhythm section. It's one of the best songs on the album, aside from the well-known singles. Unusually, Terrana's mix is longer (by 20 seconds) than the Chic original mix. The strings are simply stunning, the quickly plucked notes echoing the heartbreak in Ross's vocals on the choruses. There is also a second strings part playing chords for added texture.

The verses are less edgy than the choruses, with Ross conveying a more soulful ache. She's still sad at her loss, but there's no nervous energy about it. There's a nice section from 2:07 where the second strings part is dominant. Ross sounds terrific singing with them as they are faded up in the mix. Then, at 2:56, the strings drop away to the plucked notes and the basic rhythm. As Sammy Figueroa missed this session, it must be Tony Thompson playing the wood scraper block (a guiro) that stands out in the rhythm.

The original Chic mix lacks the echo on Edwards' bass and Ross's vocal is noticeably different. She isn't double-tracked and she sounds more up close and personal and higher in the mix. It's an interesting approach because the strings are less effective than on Terrana's mix. Overall, the Chic mix is the better one, but it would have been even better if the strings were mixed higher.

'Give Up'

This is a weak, party-style tune that does nobody any favours. The backing vocals come in first and suggest it's going to be a powerful lead vocal to follow, but when Ross comes in, it loses conviction. Without the backing vocal, she doesn't sound strong enough and it doesn't suit her vocal range; it would have been better-suited to someone like Kathy Sledge, for example, who would have given this an r&b, gutsy feel. The backing track is forceful with stabbing strings adding to the tension and a piano shadowing Ross's vocal line. Yet, it doesn't quite convince me and it just isn't interesting enough. The exception is Rodgers' guitar solo at 2:10, which is a masterful, tasty jazz workout and a highlight of both the song and the album. Sadly, the outro following it goes on for too long with little merit.

The original Chic mix is about the same length, but is smoother, and the reduced dynamics make it flow better. However, by contrast, the breakdown section at 2:54 has far more clarity in this mix.

King Of The World (Sheila & B. Devotion) (1980)

Personnel:
Sheila: lead vocals
Nile Rodgers: guitar
Bernard Edwards: bass
Tony Thompson: drums, percussion
Fonzi Thornton, Alfa Anderson, Luci Martin, Michelle Cobbs: harmony and backing vocals
Sammy Figueroa: percussion
Ray Jones: keyboards, Fender Rhodes
Andy Schwartz: piano
Cheryl Hong, Karen Milne, Marianne Carroll: the Chic strings
Gene Orloff: concert master
Larry Alexander: additional keyboards on 'King Of The World'
Produced and arranged by Bernard Edwards and Nile Rodgers, 1979
Release date: 27 June 1980
Label: Carrere/Warner Bros.
Highest chart places: UK: did not chart, US: did not chart
Running time: 34:31
All songs by Edwards and Rodgers.

The collaboration with Bette Midler had fallen through, to the chagrin of Rodgers, who told *Billboard* in December 1979 that 'We wanted to work with a white artist so people could stop tagging us as black producers or disco producers.' Sheila (born Annie Chancal) was a white artist, but she came with low expectations as a commercial proposition. She had become a star in her native France, most recently with her backing singers and dancers, the Black Devotion (shortened to B. Devotion). This had seen her chart with two disco singles ('Singin' In The Rain' and 'Light My Fire'), both inoffensive fluff at best. She was surely not on their list of singers they would like to work with, but they took up the invitation to work with her for a one-off single released in November 1979. This was one of their absolute classics in 'Spacer'. It did so well that Carrere Records asked for an album. What they got actually deviates considerably from 'Spacer' and is more the kind of album that Debbie Harry should have veered more towards on *Kookoo*. It would have suited her down to the ground.

Recording the album presented certain challenges. First and foremost, Sheila was not by any stretch of the imagination a gifted singer. Rodgers and Edwards were careful to get the best from her and try not to leave her voice exposed on any of the tracks. Even so, her delivery and lack of range are noticeable. At her very best, on 'Spacer', her glacial diction is an asset in contrast to what is easily one of Chic's best grooves.

It's a mixed styles album, with three songs from a disco background in 'Spacer', 'Don't Go' and 'Your Love Is Good', while the rest veer towards the rockier sides of *Real People* or *Kookoo.* 'Spacer' is the classic – nothing else comes close to its hypnotic brilliance. The best version of the album is the 2020 double CD edition on Warner Bros., which features all the different mixes and outtakes.

'Spacer'

One of Chic's greatest songs. It may be one of the most lyrically trite songs they ever recorded, but it is saved by the outstanding music and Sheila's ice-cool vocals, which are perfect against the relentless groove. She is supported by the choir on the choruses, but it's just her French-accented solo vocal on the verses and it works really well. The best version is on the album, two and a half magical minutes longer than the single, and it's that version we are referencing.

It's stunning right from the intro, with the piano melody cascading like fine rain. The piano is constantly and gorgeously evident, contrasting against the never-ending rhythm track. Rodgers' solo (at 3:00) is an edgy, angular, echo-drenched affair rather than a lush melody and it was exactly the right call. After a short interlude, it's straight into the breakdown at 3:57, which is amazingly good. There's still echo used on Rodgers guitars, while Thompson and Figeuroa (on shakers) keep the rhythm going, giving Edwards scope to roam around the soundscape. It's Figeuroa's metronomic shaker groove that impresses me most. He says:

> I just played through the whole thing; the idea was just to lift it up. That shaker that I played on all those records is a huge, massive shaker that was made for me by this guy in New York and it's still in my possession. I have been using it for 40 years and Chaka Khan sat on it by mistake when we did 'I'm Every Woman'. I said to her, 'Chaka, you sat on my shaker, what the fuck?!' I had to straighten it out but it still has the seal of approval from Chaka's butt!'

Ray Jones' keyboards are the first to come back in after the breakdown, followed by the strings and then the choir for the usual choruses to the fade-out.

It was edited for single release and got to number 18 in the UK chart and deserved to do a lot better than that. Alcazar had a slightly bigger hit in 2001 (it reached number 13) with 'Crying At The Discotheque', which made heavy use of 'Spacer's killer melody.

There are some interesting related mixes and outtakes of the song. 'Spacer (Outtake 1)' is 4:50 of heaven, the rhythm section (minus Figueroa) plus Jones working through the main riff and melody. 'Spacer (Outtake 2)' (1:33) starts with Thompson being told to play louder and harder, and we then get the same combination playing it through with more energy.

Remixes are such personal choices and there are four on the 2020 set. Tom Moulton's fascinating mix (9:56) pushes the piano and strings up for a lusher approach. Rodgers' verse guitar part is also way up in the mix. The first chorus is sung purely by the Chic singers. Sheila then appears in the first verse. Moulton softens her voice so she sounds like gossamer against the strings and he maintains that throughout the song. He finds an extra keyboard part for the outro, which is a delightful, unexpected bonus.

Monsieur Willy's 'Dub Version' (6:44) loses the heart of the song. Much better is his 'Rework' (4:15), which is outstanding. He takes the elements and works them into a more stately, airy, light jazz track. It's dominated by piano, Fender Rhodes and keyboards and loses the pulsing Thompson/Edwards/Figuroa groove. He leaves in Rodgers' solo, which leaps out of the mix as the only element to break the mood. The 'Freak Out Remix' (12:04) loses the focus and energy of the original; for example, the false intro lasts until 2:35 when a spoken 'one-two' kicks the song off properly. The strings are much louder, which doesn't quite work because they distract from the rest of the instrumentation. Where it really works is at 6:20 when the breakdown comes in. It has such strong clarity, with some vocal interjections and a swirling keyboard effect. When the piano leads back in from the breakdown, that dynamic clarity is retained and this makes for a strong, vibrant soundscape with some *Psycho* sounding string scrapes added later for good measure.

'Mayday'

This is a strong song with a choppy, catchy rhythm. It's the main one that makes me think of Debbie Harry, who would have sounded great on this song, but in fairness to her, Sheila doesn't let herself down on it, either. Rodgers' rhythm part imitates Morse code while the lyrics make reference to the Nato Phonetic (spelling) Alphabet in the song, as in 'Papa, Zulu, X-ray'. As Sheila desperately implores someone to 'rescue me', Rodgers comes in at 1:45 with a shrill, scintillating solo with a wobbly effect to enhance it, as though it is struggling to cut through the airwaves. It's as off-kilter as the song itself and an extraordinary piece of work, which Rodgers keeps going all the way to the full-stop outro of Sheila intoning 'baby'.

'Charge Plates And Credit Cards'

The lyrics adopt a similar approach to 'Mayday'; this time, Sheila gets to name-check credit cards. Rodgers' rocking guitar riff (with Thompson's heavy drums) in the intro is a surprise, but order is soon restored at the 14-second mark when the keyboards come in to inject a lighter, poppier touch. Rodgers doesn't switch from the riff, but he is faded lower in the mix so he blends in more, allowing Sheila the space for her vocals. She is good in the chorus, with the Chic harmony vocals aiding and making it an easy stretch for her. But in the verses, she struggles – it sounds too forced for her. There's a sympathetic piano part from Schwartz, but that only seems to highlight how poor her vocals are.

The Rodgers/Edwards twin solo/break at 2:39 is a welcome touch and warm diversion, which I always hope lasts longer than 29 seconds. But with a turnaround from Thompson, it's back to the main melody and the chorus. As it hurtles to the outro, Rodgers leads the way, and he tops that off by closing alone with a monstrous, heavy riff.

'Misery'

With the fastest tempo, this is a very poor piece. You can't blame Sheila for this one; she doesn't get a grip on it, but there's nothing much for her to work with. There are some nice chord changes in the verses, but the vocal delivery is remarkably throwaway and lightweight, especially in the choruses. This is at odds with the angst present in the lyrics. In some ways, the song reminds me of a less convincing 'I'm So Excited' by The Pointer Sisters, especially Schwartz's piano part. The song stops, and then back comes Rodgers, alone, for a thrashed, out-of-tune chord that fades out – the most interesting part of the song.

'King Of The World'

This suits Sheila's voice well. In the chorus, she is tuneful and blends well against the lurching rhythm. In the verses, she pretty much talks her way through, but it does give the words more emphasis without her having to attempt anything too tuneful. The break (2:45) is a solo from Rodgers, which sees him playing the melody and letting fly with flurries of notes.

It was released as an edited single. The 2020 album reissue includes a 6:07 outtake and a 'Club Remix' by Fred Falke. The instrumental outtake is the band running through the song in a more relaxed vein, and to me, it sounds like a stronger song and is easier to digest and enjoy, albeit overlong. Falke's mix, however, is relentlessly fatiguing in its high-energy approach.

'Cover Girls'

The band keep this one muscular and tight, but it's a vocal disaster – it just doesn't suit Sheila at all. It feels like filler, and there's no solo or breakdown for some diversion.

Somewhat amazingly, the 2020 edition includes an outtake and a remix! The instrumental outtake (2:46) sees the band running through the tune, which sounds better without vocals. The 'Extended Strings Mix' is a shock, managing to justify itself over five minutes! The addition of the strings makes an enormous difference to the verses, softening the sound and adding extra texture. Spoiling us even more, we get a breakdown at 2:26! Edwards leads it over drums, handclaps and strings. You can also hear Rodgers (otherwise missing) bleeding through in the background until he is faded up. The outro is an intense instrumental juggernaut and quite fabulous. All in all, the string mix is a more satisfying take of the song and is the go-to version.

'Your Love Is Good'

The Chic strings are here, and the song as a whole has some classic Chic hallmarks in the engaging melody lines and the tight rhythm track. Sheila is supported in the choruses by the Chic singers, but she handles the verses alone – it just doesn't work. It's a classy song, but wasted for this project. Rodgers' exuberant, jazzy solo is the high point.

There is an American promo single version, which was unreleased until the 2006 deluxe edition. This takes the song closer to Chic with the softer mix. The verses see an echo used on Sheila's voice, which is superfluous, but overall, this is much better. The instrumental outtake (2:45) is an enjoyable run-through, with Rodgers' rhythm work to the fore.

There are two remixes of the song. Dimitri From Paris's mix is musically excellent, with the strings getting a welcome boost and changing the song's arrangement considerably as a result. Does it justify being extended to 6:23? Amazingly, that's a big yes, with a terrific, extended Rodgers solo, Edwards' bass growling strongly in the heart of the sound, some jazz piano and even some extra backing vocals. This is the best version of the song by far. The 'Young Pulse' remix is also effective, featuring some wonderful jazz piano.

'Don't Go'

This was the B-side to 'Spacer', which is where it should have stayed. Sheila's almost sunny vocal is odd and goes utterly against the theme of the lyrics, which focus on the shock of a breakup. Her reassurances – 'I just hope it's understood, You call me, Anytime you want my love' – come across a little limp, and it just sounds like the kind of euro disco fluff that cropped up in the charts around this era. The Chic strings feature prominently in the chorus, but all they do is follow the melody – it's not enough. Edwards injects some nice licks and there is a breakdown of sorts from 2:55, which features Rodgers, Edwards, Thompson and Figueroa grooving along together on the main rhythm, with Rodgers high in the mix. It's the best part of the song by a long way. This is a disappointing end to the album. Fred Falke's strident 'Club Remix' on the 2020 edition fails to improve the song.

Real People (Chic) (1980)

Personnel:
Nile Rodgers: guitar, backing vocals
Bernard Edwards: bass, backing vocals, lead vocals on '26'
Tony Thompson: drums, percussion
Alfa Anderson: lead vocals on 'I Got Protection' and 'Chip Off The Old Block', backing vocals
Luci Martin: lead vocals on 'Real People', 'I Loved You More' and 'Rebels Are We', backing vocals
Fonzi Thornton: lead vocals on 'You Can't Do It Alone', backing vocals
Michelle Cobbs: backing vocals
Sammy Figueroa: percussion
Ray Jones, Andy Schwartz: keyboards, clavinet
Cheryl Hong, Karen Milne, Valerie Haywood: the Chic strings
Gene Orloff: concert master
Produced and arranged by Bernard Edwards and Nile Rodgers at Power Station, New York, in 1980
Release date: 30 June 1980
Label: Atlantic
Highest chart places: UK: did not chart, US: 30
Running time: 37:03
All songs by Edwards and Rodgers.

The label publicised the album as 'The new Chic sound for the 80s is here!' It did see the band taking steps to move on from the sound that had made them famous. Edwards had pointed towards a new direction when he told Paul Grein of *Billboard* on 15 December 1979 that he and Rodgers planned to 'get back to writing heavier ballads, rock and r&b.' It was on *Real People* where this came to fruition. On the title track, for example, Rodgers' blistering guitar solo (one of many on the album) would give many rock guitarists a run for their money. Rodgers singled out 'Real People' and 'Rebels Are We' as being two that evoked the Big Apple Band. Missing from those days was Rob Sabino, who was away working with the Simms Brothers.

Those wanting some of Rodgers' more familiar styles will enjoy the old-school 'Open Up', where he shows off his jazz chops. Then, there is his exquisite flamenco guitar part on 'You Can't Do It Alone'. 'I Loved You More', meanwhile, is firmly in the style of the previous big ballads.

Overall, it's a strong album, a consistent set of songs that stand up against the generally accepted peak of *C'est Chic* and *Risqué.* The production is excellent, too, maybe the best on all their albums, with a richness and clarity that shows the songs off beautifully. The cover, while a strong image, doesn't resonate with the title, which suggested something more revealing, stark and honest.

Chic toured America to support the album, and the string section went along, too. The band, visually just Rodgers, Edwards, Thompson, Anderson and Martin, appeared on 1 September on the *Miss America* (1981) beauty pageant performing 'Good Times'. While they are miming, this is an enthralling performance, in particular the compelling moves of Martin and Rodgers. Karen Milne logs that the string section were present for this recording, but they aren't in the footage.

'Open Up'

This is a classic bravura opening instrumental from Chic, but not entirely representative of the album. The strings take the lead on this – angular, strong and dominant, playing against Rodgers' dazzling jazzy guitar figures. This reaches an apex in the bridge section, where the trade-offs between the strings and Rodgers are stunning. It's an accomplished piece of work, perhaps the best Chic instrumental. You have to love the full stop ending, too – just a short pause and a 'Wooh, easy Dip' from Rodgers to Thompson ('Dip' was his nickname) and straight into the title track.

'Real People'

We are right into a hard-hitting Rodgers lead guitar part over a fairly straight-forward rhythm track before we're straight into the chorus. Lyrically, it's a statement of where the band were at. The bitter lyrics hit home in a way not heard before on their records, dwelling on 'folks who just can't get involved'. Commenting on the hypocrisy and phoney nature of relationships and wanting to be with 'Real People', it reveals just how burnt out Rodgers and Edwards were getting with the music industry. While the choruses are an ensemble affirmation of intent, it's down to Martin alone, with her rich, creamy voice, to deliver the details of the situation in the verses.

The guitar solo is stunning and contains a little secret. Rodgers recalled in the *Very Best Of Chic* notes in 2000 that 'as artists, we were crying for acceptance. In the middle of my guitar solo, I start playing the melody to 'I Want Your Love'. It's actually quite sad and poignant because that's how we felt. We kept thinking, 'How come everybody hates us?" Rodgers' guitar work is tougher than we are used to and his lead parts have real bite and venom. This is an extraordinary piece, with everything laid bare, almost confessionally, and put right out in front of the listener. It is one of Chic's greatest achievements. The single release got to number 79 in America.

'I Loved You More'

This is a classic ballad with a beautiful lead vocal from Martin. She sounds on the verge of tears at times, such is the conviction in her voice. Her big moment comes at 1:48 with the verse 'Now I know you've known, other lost souls like me, That lived their lives, in search of peaches and cream.' She gives it full measure, and when she pleads a little later to 'rescue me', you can really feel her desperation! Her plea cues up a sad, bluesy, stinging rock guitar solo from Rodgers that works well, but it might have been better with one of his jazzier solos. The outro is beautifully done with a real sense of resolution as Anderson pleads for the last time that 'I loved you more' over a hugely satisfying big chordal finish. You feel that all has been said; there is nothing else to say. This is just behind 'At Last I Am Free' as one of the great Chic ballads.

'I Got Protection'

This was salvaged from the *Diana* album sessions, apparently rejected by Ross – Anderson sings it instead. It's a tight, hard-hitting, r&b-flavoured piece that fits in with the tougher edges evident on this album. The choruses are ensemble vocals with the strings adding great enhancement. While this suits the Chic style, it would have left Ross fighting for her space.

The line 'monkey see and monkey do' (1:47) is a Jamaican saying dating back to the 18th century, which approximately means 'learning a process – without necessarily understanding why it works – by imitation' as the song makes quite clear. Rodgers' solo (3:41) is at first another in keeping with the rockier' tone he uses on the album. Jones or Schwartz (the credits don't specify who) plays a funky clavinet part behind him as he solos away. The song finds a new lease of life from Rodgers' solo onward, as he progresses more into jazzy territory. Overall, another strong offering.

'Rebels Are We'

Rodgers, in the *Very Best Of Chic* notes in 2000, saw it as a throwback: '(It) is exactly what we were writing when we were the Big Apple Band: millions of chord changes, interesting licks, weird tonalities.' This is another one with a harder feel. Martin gets to sing the verses – she has such an expressive voice, which suits the 'up close and personal' arrangement. The chorus is more expansive with ensemble vocals (as ever).

The sharp, darting bow work from the strings gives the song excitement. Rodgers gets his solo at 2:26, a melodic riff on the main melody line, which he backs with another rhythm part. It's an average track, mostly brightened up by Rodgers' solo and Martin's voice in the verses. It was released as a single and got to number 61 in America.

'Chip Off The Old Block'

Anderson is back on lead vocals for this one, which is the first of a pair of very 'trad' Chic songs. It's a spritely, chugging track with an insistent handclap percussion track. Anderson sings the verses alone but is joined by the other vocalists for the uninspiring chorus, which lets the song down. Apart from Anderson, the big plaudits must go to the strings; the section from 2:51, with the dramatic clipped notes (playfully sounding like chips being cut off), is excellent, interwoven with those big, soaring sweeps they do so well.

'26'

The lyrics are a reference to the Bo Derek film *10* – 'On a scale of one to ten my baby's a 26' – and they manage to deliver the ensemble chorus endearingly well. Edwards' curiously subdued solo vocal verses somehow work out well as a contrast. The music is much better, led by a supremely catchy guitar riff. The light, skipping melodies and the warm groove are infectious and fun. The breakdown comes in quite late (3:05) and is rooted in the strings playing off Edwards and Thompson before Rodgers leads the way back a mere 12 seconds later. It's brief but fabulous – as is the whole song. This is a 'typical' old-school type Chic track and is hard to resist, so don't try!

'You Can't Do It Alone'

Thornton's first solo Chic vocal was a memorable moment for him. He recalled to *PopMatters* on 11 December 2020:

> Nile said, 'Fonzi, I got a song for you for our next album.' I was ecstatic. He played it on the guitar and it was just gorgeous. He showed me the melody and said, 'Now, just make it your own.' When we went on tour that summer, they gave me a solo spot on their show. I remember I was wearing a short red leather jacket and some big, black leather pants and I would come down to the front of the stage and sing 'You Can't Do It Alone' and everybody would love it.

Lyrically, it's a regretful 'break-up' song. His voice is good and has a naturally higher register than the more limited Edwards. In essence, this is the kind of song that would have also suited Anderson, with whom he blends so well on the choruses.

Rodgers signs off the song and the album in style with dazzling 'flamenco' style guitar passages from 3:38. He overlays at least two guitar parts, dovetailing with each other in what is a gorgeous outro. This is a nice showcase for Thornton, who deserved the spotlight.

Don't Throw My Love Away (Fonzi Thornton) (Unreleased, 1980)

Confirmed personnel:
Fonzi Thornton: lead vocals, backing vocals
Alfa Anderson, Luci Martin, Michelle Cobbs: backing vocals
Nile Rodgers: guitar
Bernard Edwards: bass
Tony Thompson: drums
Sammy Figueroa: percussion
Cheryl Hong, Karen Milne, Valerie Haywood: the Chic strings
Produced and arranged by Bernard Edwards and Nile Rodgers, between September and October 1980
All songs by Edwards and Rodgers.

Thornton recalled to *PopMatters* on 11 December 2020 that it was 'shortly after the *Real People* album that they started saying, 'Fonzi, we're going to sign you to our production company and we're going to get this deal.' They wrote eight songs and we just went at it. They gave me the songs to take home because they said, 'We want you to create your performances and then come in and sing.' It showed that they respected my talent.' Thornton also named some of the contributors to the album. One he missed was Sammy Figueroa, but he confirms that, 'Yes, I played on that album.' A sign of how far Rodgers and Edwards' star had waned was that they couldn't get a label to pick up the album. But it wasn't necessarily the songs that were a problem. Thornton recalled to Daryl Easlea that RCA had passed on it because of the hefty price tag.

Rodgers and Edwards copyrighted the album title and songs at the US Copyright Office. Document number V1848P104 lists the eight songs in alphabetical order as 'Don't Throw My Love Away', 'Frostbite', 'Hold It', 'I Can Love', 'I'll Change My Game', 'I Work For A Living', 'Riding' and 'Who Me?' Two were officially released on *Savoir Faire* and an edit of 'I Work For A Living' had already made it out in 1982 on the *Soup For One* soundtrack.

Karen Milne logs a recording session for the strings on 23 October 1980. Assuming 'normal' Chic recording practices, I would speculate the album was likely put together, start to finish, between September and October 1980. The other session players would almost certainly include one or more of Sabino, Schwartz and Jones on keyboards.

Thornton eventually got his solo deal. It was RCA who relented, but it was for a whole new album – *The Leader* (1983).

'I'll Change My Game'

A haunting piano intro gives way to Rodgers' chattering guitar and we are off. Thornton quickly proves he is an excellent lead singer as well as a great backing/harmony vocalist. It's a positive, life-affirming track, but could have done with stronger dynamic variation between the verses and chorus. Musically, it's undercooked; you wait for someone to break cover for a solo, but there really isn't anything of note. It's pleasant enough and was released on the *Savoir Faire* set.

'I Work For A Living'

The version on *Soup For One* was 3:31, but Rodgers mixed a 7:02 edit for *Savoir Faire*. As that is more likely to be how it was intended, we will focus on the longer cut.

Thornton's voice blends well with the backing vocals on the chorus, as it should, of course (he is likely on backups too). The verses are pretty minimal and feature Thornton alone. He sounds good singing solo, but the backing track isn't that different to the chorus, which feels lazy.

The big problem is that this is an average Chic song. The instrumental break at 3:15 is the best part of it – basically, Edwards grooves on the bass with a strong rhythm from Rodgers and Thompson (plus handclaps). Sabino gets to add some dribbly sounding synth runs, which don't add much to the sound other than take your attention away from the rhythm.

I Love My Lady (Johnny Mathis) (1981)

Personnel:
Johnny Mathis: lead vocals
Nile Rodgers: guitar
Bernard Edwards: bass
Tony Thompson: drums
Sammy Figueroa: percussion (uncredited)
Ray Jones, Rob Sabino, Andy Schwartz: keyboards
Alfa Anderson, Luci Martin, Fonzi Thornton, Michelle Cobbs: backing vocals
Cheryl Hong, Karen Milne, Valerie Haywood: the Chic strings
Produced and arranged by Bernard Edwards and Nile Rodgers at Power Station, New York, between December 1980 and February 1981
Release date: 8 December 2017 (*Voice Of Romance* box set), then stand-alone on 21 April 2018
Label: Columbia
Highest chart places: UK: did not chart, US: did not chart
Running time: 38:32
All songs by Edwards and Rodgers.

Mathis's management made the initial call to Rodgers and Edwards. One imagines that on the back of the Diana Ross album, they thought the duo could conjure up the same magic for Mathis. Her album had been subject to a controversial remix to get it out, but perhaps Mathis's management were unaware of this. In the end, it was deja vu for Rodgers and Edwards as the album was confined to Columbia's vaults. The label had Mathis down as a popular singer, mostly of romantic ballads, and in a largely mainstream style. The selling point for them was his voice and his clear diction and phrasing. On this album, he works with the band, who frequently get the space for instrumental sections, and his phrasing is tailored to fit the material. It's still Mathis, but not as Columbia wanted him, and they believed his fan base wouldn't support it. Rodgers accurately described the album in Daryl Easlea's biography as 'Al Jarreau meets Chic. It didn't sound like Johnny Mathis to me; it was a little more edgy than I'd ever heard him.' It is true that it's very much a Chic album with Johnny Mathis on lead vocals, but he is absolutely brilliant and the partnership works.

Guide vocals for Mathis to work to were laid down prior to his arrival for the sessions by Fonzi Thornton. Mathis then recorded his vocals over four sessions between 23 December 1980 and 21 January 1981. He pointed out to Charles Donovan for *PopMatters* in April 2019 that changes were still being made while he was there:

> They were making up melodies as we went along in the studio. It was a process that was different from the recordings I had done up to that time. There was a lot of stopping and starting and stopping and starting.

> Conversations would be, 'Maybe we would like to say this in the song, maybe we would like to say that in the song' and they would change the song right there and then. It was not like anything I'd done before, on-the-spot improvisation.

The strings were added later, recorded in tandem with Debbie Harry's *KooKoo.* We know this because Karen Milne's diary highlights the first date for the strings sessions on 24 February 1981. A day earlier, they were working for the first time on *KooKoo.* After just one day on the Mathis session, the string players went back to recording overdubs on *KooKoo.*

What the album lacked was an obvious big hit single, but it does work really well as an album. It's a cohesive piece of work and the standard of the songs is consistently very good to excellent, all topped off with Mathis's assured, superb vocals. He was pleased with the experience, commenting, again, to Donovan:

> I have a great deal of fondness for Nile Rodgers and Bernard Edwards. Over the years, I've loved their music, and what we did in the studio was really quite experimental. It was fun. I enjoyed it. I remember they sent a limousine for me every day to go to the studio and I thought that was a big deal. I think it holds up quite nicely as far as what's going on musically with young kids today.

The first three songs appeared on the *Savoir Faire* set in 2010. The full album finally emerged in 2017 as part of *The Voice Of Romance: The Columbia Original Album Collection.* It achieved a standalone release (by Legacy Recordings) for Record Store Day on 21 April 2018, soon followed by a CD release. It's an album and one that deserves its belated acclaim.

'Fall In Love (I Want To)'

This superb song should have got the nod to be a single. It instantly sounds like Chic and is firmly in the tradition of their classic ballads. The strings are the perfect backing for Mathis, soaring at the end of each line of the chorus. The accents they play in the verses are sublime. Equally as brilliant as Mathis is Rodgers' carefully picked guitar parts, which are the perfect melodic counterpoint. But in the end, this is all about Mathis, who delivers a masterclass in phrasing. Then, there's the incredible note he holds on 'love' at 4:36 for 27 seconds – astonishing! Mathis gets a real sense of yearning into his delivery, as though love is, and will remain, just out of reach.

'It's Alright To Love Me'

The song was originally titled 'Go With The Flow', and that sums up the second half of the song. It's one that would have given the record label palpitations; it's very unlike Mathis's normal style at all. The bright and sunny piano intro is a great start. The song is quite staccato in construction and rhythm, with the piano adding the sweet counterpoint melody of the song's main musical motif. The section that would have tipped it for the label comes in just after the piano melody echoes the intro at 2:06. Here, the backing vocalists come in next, singing 'go with the flow' in unison. A final 'go' from them ushers in an instrumental break. This break is full-on Chic, with Rodgers and Edwards in full flight with an absolutely terrific piano line over the top. But Mathis is completely absent until he comes back in with the backing vocalists at 3:09! With and without him, it all makes for a magical last two minutes of the song.

'Something To Sing About'

This opens strongly as a Chic track with a staccato rhythm from Rodgers before Mathis enters with the backing singers as part of a chorus. It's very Chic, and softens his way into the song. The call and response from then on between Mathis and the backing vocalists is top quality, one of the best examples in the Chic repertoire of a lead vocalist working with backing vocalists. It leaves Mathis with the verses to showcase his vocals, and there are only two – both in the first half of the song!

To make it worse, or better, there are other sections where Mathis isn't one of the featured vocalists such as 2:15 – 'sing, sing' etc. – where Fonzi Thornton leads the ladies, with Anderson and Martin audibly popping up out of the choir. You keep expecting Mathis to come back in, but he doesn't. 'Where's Johnny?', you can imagine the exasperated label bosses asking. But this is a fine ending to a great song, even without him.

'I Love My Lady'

Sammy Figueroa's percussion takes centre stage for the intro on this beautiful samba-style track. Rodgers' jazzy/flamenco guitar works well against Mathis. The backing rhythm track is light and sparse, with Figeuroa's congas and a bubbly bass part from Edwards. The result is that Mathis is prominent in the mix, with even the backing vocalists distant. It picks up at 2:36 with the strings entering, while the song retains its light, melodic feel, dancing all the way to the outro.

'Take Me'

The chorus is rather dull and flat-sounding, but the verses are much better with a punchy, choppy rhythm and a precise vocal from Mathis. There is a short instrumental break (3:30), but this, like the chorus, lacks in inspiration, being more of an interlude. Fortunately, things pick up at 4:12 with a more vibrant and dramatic variation on the vocals and melody, with dazzling strings. Unfortunately, the backing singers almost drown out Mathis in the outro!

'Judy'

Mathis pleads for his lady not to go, but, of course, she does. This is one of those upbeat Chic songs that still manages to have a sad twist to the music.

It's not especially a good song, but it isn't bad either. The vocal work from Mathis and the backing singers is solid, but the instrumental track feels a bit limited in scope. I like the clavinet part (which always seems to spice up a song), likely played by Sabino. It's the shortest track on the album (at 3:30), which isn't too surprising considering the limited ambition in the arrangement. To stretch it out longer would have required a breakdown or instrumental break and the song would have benefited from that.

'Stay With Me'

This is much better. It has a strong, piano-driven melody line, which sits well with Rodgers' ever-present guitar licks. The piano wraps around Mathis, adding embellishments and flourishes to his lines when appropriate. It's one of my favourite piano parts on any Chic or Chic-related track. It's a simple, yet very moving song with Mathis getting quite emotional in his delivery.

'Love And Be Loved'

They finish off with a catchy pop tune that highlights the band, who play it tight and extremely catchy, with the keyboard melody providing the hook. Edwards is superb with his wandering runs and the little licks he puts in for enhancement. Mathis isn't as effective as he has been, but he has little to do. The chorus suits him well enough vocally, but it's lyrically mundane, with little more than the title to it. He seems a bit rushed in the two verses, with an almost nervous, hesitant tone in his voice. Despite that, there is an energy and quality in the band performance that satisfies.

KooKoo (Debbie Harry) (1981)

Personnel:
Debbie Harry: lead vocals
Chris Stein: guitar
Nile Rodgers: guitar, vocals on 'Backfired'
Bernard Edwards: bass
Tony Thompson: drums
Fonzi Thornton: backing vocals
Ray Jones, Rob Sabino: keyboards
Sammy Figueroa, Manola Badrena, Roger Squitero: percussion
Cheryl Hong, Karen Milne, Valerie Haywood: the Chic strings (uncredited)
Vinny Della Rocca: saxophone
Ray Maldonado: trumpet
Nathaniel S. Hardy Jnr.: keyboards
Gerald Casale, Mark Mothersbaugh, Gordon Grody: backing vocals
Chuck Martin: dog bark
Produced and arranged at The Power Station, New York, by Bernard Edwards and Nile Rodgers, in the spring of 1981
Release date: 27 July 1981
Label: Chrysalis
Highest chart places: UK: 6, US: 25
Running time: 42:27

When Blondie decided to take some time apart from each other in 1981, it was to Chic that Debbie Harry and her partner, Chris Stein, gravitated. The couple first met Rodgers and Edwards in 1979 when they called into the Power Station while Blondie were recording *Eat To The Beat*. Stein was so enamoured that he suggested they produce the next Blondie album (*AutoAmerican*). That didn't come together, so they worked again with Mike Chapman. The album spawned the hit single 'Rapture', which audibly revealed their appreciation of Chic.

About five weeks were spent on recording and overdubs. Karen Milne logged the first day of the string overdub sessions as 23 February 1981, with two further days on 25 and 26 February. This is interesting because the Chic strings are not credited on the album. They are not on many tracks, and when they are, as on 'Backfired', they are so low and blended in that they might as well not have been used at all.

In theory, the combination of Harry and Stein, plus Chic, should have been unbeatable. Rodgers saw their role this way when speaking on *Freeze Frame* in 1981: 'We have to understand what Debbie's about in order to write songs that represent Debbie's image.' On the same show, Harry gave her view of the collaboration:

> As musicians, we've all sort of evolved through the same period and we've been locked and identified into a certain groove. And now we all want to do

> something to get us out into another area and this is the opportunity. They are doing a lot of things in rock 'n' roll which they have never been able to do. By writing music for me, they are able to approach my audience, which is more of a rock audience, so the music is tougher, which is better for me because I was getting limited by this cutesy-pop business and I wanted to do like a rougher kind of rock music.

In spite of the positive intentions, the project suffered because the styles of Harry/Stein and Chic were not a good fit – they tend to clash. This disjointedness was enhanced by three writing partnerships. There's a difference in the feel between the Harry/Stein compositions and those written by Rodgers/Edwards. Those partnerships share four songs each, with two as compositions by all four. For me, it would have flowed better with the partnerships split to a side each and 'Under Arrest' closing a Harry/Stein side and 'Oasis' closing a Rodgers/Edwards side.

The best songs are all by Rodgers/Edwards, but even so, Harry doesn't sound assured or convincing with the Chic form and style. Whereas they managed to accommodate Sheila for her album, they don't seem able to give Harry a similarly comfortable platform. She often sounds exposed in the mix, and her voice is not strong enough to carry the songs. It's an album that had lots of promise, which, frustratingly, it rarely comes close to fulfilling. Sammy Figueroa tactfully sums up the album as 'kind of a weird record.'

But Chrysalis initially must have thought they had a winner, packaged inside a probably expensive cover. H. R. Giger (of *Alien* fame) customised Brian Aris's photo. Chris Stein revealed in his autobiography *Under A Rock* (Corsair, 2024) that he and Harry first met Giger at a show of his *Alien* illustrations at the Hansen Gallery in New York. Giger agreed to work with the duo in the future. Giger picked up on the album's punning title reference, sending initial sketches of Harry's face pierced by Kuku safety pins, and suggesting an acupuncture/punk referenced image. The final image with the steampunk style shot was certainly attention-grabbing.

The promotion campaign came unstuck as soon as 'Backfired' was released as the pre-album single in July 1981. It only reached number 32 in the UK singles chart and number 43 in America. David Hepworth pithily observed in *Smash Hits* that 'If this is the best that *KooKoo* has to offer, then Debbie Harry's solo career is going to be short.' He wasn't wrong.

The final snub came with the second single release from the album. 'The Jam Was Moving' made it to just number 82 in the UK. 'Chrome' was tried out as the third single, but notably not in America nor the UK, where the record companies had clearly decided enough was enough. It would be five years before her next solo album, *Rockbird*. It featured a glimmer of Chic involvement with Rodgers co-writing (but not playing on) the closing track 'Beyond The Limit'.

'Jump Jump' (Harry/Stein)
A lot of energy here, but not much of note to show for it. The production is dry and Harry's vocals are quite exposed, with no backing singers until the second half to offset her strident, limited delivery. The guitar solo in the bridge, by Stein, disappoints and never really gets going. But Harry comes back in with a softer, more effective vocal and picks up on her delivery. She sounds much stronger and more confident in the second half. The backing vocals help her a lot here, too. In spite of that second-half recovery, this is still a poor effort.

'The Jam Was Moving' (Edwards/Rodgers)
This quirky stop/start rhythm track also has an effective keyboard melody. Top marks go to Rodgers for his guitar solo, which leaps out of the backing track at you. It sounds like he has overlaid two guitar parts here, with the odd 'freaky sounding' one of them reversed. The basic rhythm track works well, with Rodgers again shining on his chugging riffs. The backing singers (Gordon Grody plus Devo's Mark Mothersbaugh and Gerald Casale) have an automated feel to them that adds a little spice to it all.

The deluxe edition of the album has an extended (5:03) mix, which doesn't add much to proceedings. Much better is the 3:32 Chris Stein and Debbie Harry remix (also on the deluxe edition), which has more snap and punch to it. It also moves a Rodgers guitar part to the intro and it works a treat, with much more presence, which is true of his part throughout. This is the best version of the song, which was originally released as the second single from the album.

'Chrome' (Harry/Stein)
Chris Stein said in *Under A Rock* that the song had been intended for the remake of Jean-Luc Godard's 1965 film *Alphaville*. It was to have starred Debbie Harry and, curiously, Robert Fripp (of King Crimson fame). The film didn't happen, but the song was resurrected for *KooKoo*.

The intro is good, with what sounds like Figueroa, Badrena and Squitero all playing congas at the same time, along with the crashing guitar chords. It goes downhill from there as soon as Harry comes in for another lacklustre vocal. The backing is low in the mix, so she stands out, but she just can't carry the tune in a melodic or interesting way. It's probably Stein who plays the classic rock guitar solo, which is another misstep. The outro, which is a return to the musical theme of the intro, is the best part of this woeful song.

'Surrender' (Edwards/Rodgers)
This is easily Harry's best vocal on the album. She sounds completely different, with more presence; you would swear this was recorded in a different studio. She's sexy and wry and her delivery is engaging. Equally, the band are more on fire, Edwards spraying off some funky bass runs which seem to invigorate the band.

For some reason, it wasn't selected as a single, and there isn't an extended mix either, but there really should have been. This is the best track by far and would have been the perfect template for the album. More like this and it would have been a great album.

'Inner City Spillover' (Harry/Stein)
Time for some reggae now, which understandably showcases Edwards, while Rodgers plays the off-beat licks. It's limited in its ambition and Harry doesn't seem to get a handle on how best to approach the song. They don't know where to go on the instrumental break, which runs out of steam, as does the track itself. Amazingly, an extended version (5:53), adding little to shout about, was included on the deluxe edition.

'Backfired' (Edwards/Rodgers)
The intro is quite thin-sounding and the mix isn't great after that either. Rodgers sounds like he is in another room to Edwards, who is high in the mix. Meanwhile, Harry's often weak delivery on the album is at its worst here. It's Rodgers who performs the rap sections and is more credible than you might expect. The song is overlong at 4:54, but we do get a Chic breakdown of sorts when it drops down to the rhythm at 2:53, with Edwards on imperious form. It's the best part of the song, other than the actually quite clever ending as Harry intones, 'Just drop to a dead stop'. There is an extended (6:23) mix on the deluxe edition, which basically sees the breakdown/jam section expanded, allowing the band to stretch out. There is also a remix by Bruce Forrest and Frank Heller on the deluxe edition, which is very different in that it is dominated by electric piano. It's still a variation on an average song, but that piano part is excellent.

'Now I Know You Know' (Edwards/Rodgers)
This song is something of a close cousin to 'At Last I Am Free' – the chords and melody are similar, with Rodgers on similarly strong rhythm guitar throughout. The change of tempo for the outro is a nice touch and the horns are superb over the percussion tracks. This excellent song was a huge giveaway for Rodgers and Edwards because it is up there with their big ballads.

'Under Arrest' (Edwards/Harry/Rodgers/Stein)
There's a strong demo quality to this; it sounds unfinished and it's surprising to see Rodgers/Edwards on the songwriting credits. It's clear that the mash-up of two very different song-writing teams doesn't work. It's closer in style to Blondie than Chic and is a poor effort – filler at best.

'Military Rap' (Harry/Stein)
This begins with a truly horrible intro with a reveille bugle call, from which the song never really recovers. It's a Devo-style song but without their wit and

intelligence. Harry raps out the lyrics over an urgent backing track that is all bluster. It's very hard to listen to this drivel all the way through.

'Oasis' (Edwards/Harry/Rodgers/Stein)
To close the album, we have this Eastern-flavoured song with lots of percussion. Roger Squitero picks it out as a favourite of the recording sessions. He thinks that 'it's me on congas, Manola (Badrena) on talking drum, Sammy (Figeueroa) on shakers – with more shakers and a tambourine overdubbed by the three of us.' The three men immediately set the tempo and rhythmic feel of this track, with Edwards, Thompson and Rodgers adding the melody and muscle. As this doesn't test her vocal range, Harry is comfortable here and adds some nice inflections. The outro could have been longer; it starts to get even more interesting when the horns come in – there was a scorching jam just ripe for an extended mix here. This is a very decent end to the album.

Take It Off (Chic) (1981)

Personnel:
Nile Rodgers: guitar, backing vocals, lead vocals on 'Your Love Is Cancelled'
Bernard Edwards: bass, backing vocals, lead vocals on 'Flash Back', 'Take It Off' and 'Just Out Of Reach'
Tony Thompson: drums, percussion
Alfa Anderson: lead vocals on 'Would You Be My Baby' and 'Just Out Of Reach', backing vocals
Luci Martin: lead vocals on 'Stage Fright', 'Burn Hard', 'Telling Lies' and 'Take It Off', backing vocals
Fonzi Thornton, Michelle Cobbs, Jocelyn Brown: harmony and backing vocals
Sammy Figueroa, Manola Badrena, Roger Squitero: percussion
Ray Jones, Rob Sabino: keyboards, synth
Michael Brecker, Ronnie Cuber, Lenny Pickett, Vinny Della Rocca: saxophone
Randy Brecker, Ray Maldonado: trumpet, flugelhorn
Produced and arranged by Bernard Edwards and Nile Rodgers at Power Station, New York, in 1981
Release date: 16 November 1981
Label: Atlantic
Highest chart places: UK: did not chart, US: 124
Running time: 40:00
All songs by Edwards and Rodgers.

Rob Sabino returns to the fold, sharing keyboard and piano duties with Ray Jones. Sadly, there are no Chic Strings, which are much missed because they were so integral to the Chic sound.

Take It Off moves the Chic sound onto the streets in a funkier, more urban style than the glossier sounds on previous albums. This is particularly evidenced on 'Burn Hard' and 'Stage Fright'. Anderson spoke about it to Oliver Witt for *Wortwahl* in May 2022: 'I never had a conversation with Bernard and Nile about it, but listening to the album again and listening to how stripped down it was and how raw and how the strings were really replaced by those hard driving horns, I am sure that they really began to rethink the direction.'

Consequently, this album has a harder funk/rock edge than we have had before, with the Rodgers/Edwards/Thompson core rhythm section at the heart of it. Anderson and Martin are more prominent, too, with the latter taking most of the lead vocals this time. Anderson told Oliver Witt:

> When you listen to the album, Bernard and Nile definitively wanted something more raw and my vocal approach was more suitable for the earlier recordings and themes. They used strings then and my voice was soft and maybe a bit more melodic on the earlier stuff. I was a little disappointed, but I think that Luci's vocals are perfect for the songs on *Take It Off*. As producers, they were smart enough to see that.

In fact, side one features no lead vocals from Anderson, and with Edwards chipping in with several lead vocals, and even Rodgers getting one, the album was certainly ringing the changes vocally. Furthermore, there are no real ballads, which would have given Anderson or Martin more scope.

Roger Squitero is one of the three percussionists on the album. He recalls:

> Around that time, Sammy, Manolo and I were doing a lot of recording together. Word got around that we worked well together and people liked hiring us as a trio. We three seemed to be on the same page and had a sense of what the tracks needed, and we took turns playing various instruments. I honestly can't remember who played what, but we recorded all our parts at the same time, so it was three percussion parts always being done together. Nile and Bernard pretty much let us come up with our own parts, and the three of us would talk over who would play what on each track as we got to it – we overdubbed on Tony's tracks.

The cartoon cover was 'different'. Anderson observed to Oliver Witt: 'I was supposed to be the lady in the red trousers, and the one in the yellow dress is Luci. I like that cover, but I think that Luci and I were a little objectified, but that was long before I even had an opinion about women's issues and the objectification of women. But I still think it's a great cover.' Tony Wright put together the cover. He recalls how it all came to be: 'Nile Rodgers liked my *Police And Thieves* cover for Junior Murvin, and he wanted something similar for Chic. He brought the band up to my apartment, which was in New York, just around the corner from Studio 54. Nile arranged each member of the band as he wanted them to appear on the cover while I made sketches for the art.'

The album barely reached the American charts (number 124). Anderson told Oliver Witt she felt that the album's poor sales were because 'sometimes, the audience want you to give them the same things they love and know from you. And when you begin to make a departure, sometimes they go with you and sometimes they don't. And they didn't seem to go with us this time. It says in one of our earlier songs: 'Sometimes you win, sometimes you lose, take a little chance, it don't mean nothing'. So Bernard and Nile just rolled the dice.'

Chic's shining period saw their unique style imitated and adopted by others; now, on *Take It Off,* they sounded like they were copying others, following and not leading. In spite of the lack of success for the album, Chic toured on the back of it. Rob Sabino made his debut on tour with them, free at last from other commitments. One stand-out gig, in June 1981, saw Chic share the bill at Bond's Nightclub on Broadway with The Clash and Blondie.

'Stage Fright'

This track opens the album in traditional Chic style, easing you in with its familiarity. The lyrical inspiration for Rodgers was a gig he played pre-Chic at Oakland Stadium, California. There were 75,000 there and Rodgers needed a cup of beer to conquer his nerves. Anderson told Oliver Witt:

> I really do like 'Stage Fright'. It's so up-tempo and I love Luci's voice on it, and I love the chorus we did as a group with Fonzi (Thornton), Michelle (Cobbs) and Jocelyn (Brown) – they were on these sessions as well. All of us were nervous before live performances. Each of us had a little bit of stage fright. I was so nervous that my knees would actually shake and knock together. But once we got into it and were on stage, it was fine.

The strong a cappella intro is an immediate attention grabber. Then, Rodgers' skipping guitar line comes in – a really strong hook – which comes back in for every chorus. Luci Martin is terrific in the verses – powerful and still expressive. She was the right choice for the verses instead of Anderson or Edwards. For the exultant chorus, it's her plus Anderson and the three backing singers in unison.

The instrumental break (1:42) is primarily led by Edwards' bass. Frustratingly, it's the weakest part of the song, and nothing like the classic breakdowns. What we get is a simple groove of bass, keyboards and drums that only slightly picks up when Rodgers comes in. When the vocals eventually re-enter, it's for a repeat of the chorus and the verses of the first half. Had there been a stronger, more satisfying breakdown, the song would have been elevated several notches, but the vocals and that hook from Rodgers are enough to bring me back to the song

'Burn Hard'

'Slap your bass, burn hard', exhort the choral choir, and Edwards, for one, needs no further encouragement. This is a deep and dirty funk groove with the verses adding lighter dynamics. The call-and-response-style interplay between Martin and the backing vocalists is excellent. As with 'Stage Fright', group vocals for the chorus add that huge extra lift and push.

There's a surprise at 2:41 with a heavy grinding riff from Rodgers, which sees Jones or Sabino dropping back to piano to accompany him. It's a nice contrasting part of the song. The vocal mantra after it – 'Burn hard today, today get smart, smart as a fox, a fox you say' – just drips with dramatic intonation. But the best section comes at 3:35 when the vocal choir slowly intone word by word over Edwards' bass and Thompson's drums. Their diction and the bare-bones backing really makes their vocals pop out. Edwards' flourishes and licks here are dazzling and so typical of the man at his best. Piano and synth then come back in with a stuttering part from Rodgers. Unfortunately, the strident synth dominates the outro; Edwards might have been the better choice to lead it musically given his great work on the song. It's not a great song, but it's worth its place.

'So Fine'

A light, jazzy tune, with Rodgers blending at least two guitar parts for the intro melody. There is no lead vocalist as such, the vocal line being sung by the vocal choir. Lyrically, there isn't much more than the 'so fine to me' line, which punctuates the extensive instrumental extemporisations.

Sabino's synth is featured heavily, often as the lead instrument. It sounds similar to a brass arrangement but a much better option would have been to use real brass. The synth part just doesn't hit the spot. Rodgers, however, is on fine form and his guitar work is the standout. He starts working up to it at 2:03 with a tight series of licks before really stretching out at 2:38 with some marvellous jazzy runs and then reverting to more angular riffing all the way to the outro. His solo is the best part of the song and it pretty much takes up half of it!

'Flash Back'

A funky ballad, heavy on bass and drums. Lyrically this is a review of Chic's past with Edwards on lead vocals. He reflects that 'makin' love and dance was all we'd do', which is a wryly loose approximation of Chic's work. He gets the feeling of warm memories across so well in his vocals. I love the piano and keyboards phrases, too, which Sabino and/or Jones plays as accents on the vocal lines. The thoughtful nature of the lyrics would have made Anderson an obvious choice to sing it, but as this song is very much about the story of Edwards and Rodgers, it makes sense for Edwards to take the mic.

The sparking, electric punch from Martin and Anderson in the bridge at 2:14 – which tells Edwards to 'Flash back, a few years in time. Maybe then you will find, that the reason for the pleasin' was the teasin'' – is incredibly effective. It raises the temperature several notches and sizzles as Edwards asks his 'sweet sexy love' to come back to him!

Rodgers' solo (2:51) is a brooding, melodic spin around Edwards' bass pulse – and that pulse is a huge part of the song. After that solo, it's down to Edwards for his long sign-off into the distance. This is an excellent different take on the Chic sound and one of the best songs on the album.

'Telling Lies'

The intro is solidly bubbly and synth-heavy, and this melody is also a key part of the rest of the song. Apart from the intro, it's used for textures and never again as a solo instrument, which was a good decision. It's Martin again for lead vocals, although Anderson also sings some harmony parts with her. The interesting chord changes (Amin7, Emin7, A7 and Emin) and an expansive sound in the arrangement call to mind prime early Chic. However, it's undercooked at just over two and a half minutes. It's one that should have been worked on more with a bridge, breakdown or even a solo from Rodgers.

'Your Love Is Cancelled'

Rodgers gets his debut lead vocal on this limited band performance – only Rodgers, Edwards, Thompson and Sabino play on it. A catchy, finger-clicking opening hooks you in, and the stop-start rhythms of the music are equally quirky. Edwards turns in a superb bass performance; he is a marvel of melody, technique and power. By contrast, Rodgers is less obtrusive, but listen carefully and he delivers some wickedly funky licks before stepping out up front for a cheekily twitchy outro solo. Without any backing singers or a breakdown, this one could have been filler. But the blend of the four together is lively, with exquisite little touches from all of them. It's a delight for the ears and a deep cut classic, ripe and ready to be rediscovered.

'Would You Be My Baby'

Anderson gets her first lead vocal, but sadly, it's not a great cut. It could and should have been an up-tempo slice of Chic at their best, but musically, it feels too understated. Anderson is, of course, as wonderful as ever – an enormously expressive and gifted vocalist. Her effortless 'why don't you come on and be' at 2:10 is a tingling moment of pleasure amongst several moments that pepper the song. The outro, without any further contributions from Anderson, is a warm, summery, laid-back groove. It's a song that could have been much better with a more dynamic arrangement.

'Take It Off'

Martin and Edwards share the vocals on this strutting, urban affair. It kind of works as a duet, but Martin is such a powerhouse that I would have let her sing it alone. The backing vocals are used for the limited chorus, which is more of an interjection than anything. The break at 2:49 – a busy, muscular bassline from Edwards over the brass stabs and drums, which Rodgers cannot resist joining – is intense. The momentum is maintained as the vocals come back and the song sizzles all the way to the outro. It's not a classic, but it's a strong piece.

'Just Out Of Reach'

Lyrically, this was Edwards' take on the band's current situation in popular music. Rodgers expounded in the *Very Best Of Chic* notes in 2000: 'Certain things in our lives were no longer as clear as they had been in the 1970s. The 1980s were a time of transition, and a lot of things were just out of reach. The hit records were right there, but you couldn't put your finger on them.'

The muted guitar from Rodgers over a sparse backdrop sets a subdued mood. Anderson matches that with a reflective, soulful vocal that expresses her woes: 'I want a love that's mine all mine, You keep it just out of reach'. The root of the issues seems to be the falseness of fame as Rodgers and Edwards now saw it, Anderson adding that 'makin' it here seems such a cinch, but soon she'll smell the stench, of the gutter-dwellers, them pretty fellows'.

That was the female point of view, and Edwards takes over on lead vocals for the male point of view; it turns out that he is equally disconsolate – 'I sit alone and wonder why, sweet love just pass me by'. While this makes for an interesting dynamic, seeing these similar but different frustrations, it would have been a stronger song if just Anderson had taken the lead all the way through. There's an especially effective part where Anderson sings 'you keep it just out of reach' and cues in an exhilarating saxophone solo (2:01) – a great response to her voice.

'Baby Doll'

The album closes with this killer jazz instrumental. Everything seems to revolve around Edwards' formidable bass, including a wonderful brass arrangement. This really has all the musical contributors firing on all cylinders – the tenor sax solo is pure excitement and is the dominant solo instrument. Even Rodgers and Edwards don't intervene, keeping to their rhythm duties. They should have built on this track, made it longer and given Rodgers and Edwards a chance to let rip, but what there is, at just three minutes long, is breathlessly good.

Soup For One (Chic & others) (1982)

Produced by Bernard Edwards and Nile Rodgers between 1978 and 1982.
Release date: 1982
Label: Mirage
Highest chart places: UK: did not chart, US: 168
Running time: 36:46
All five new songs by Edwards and Rodgers.

The film *Soup For One* was written and directed by Jonathan Kaufer. The plot was about a New York cable television producer determined to find his ideal woman. To further his search, he has an artist's sketch made of her, as you do. Dating mishaps ensue until he finally meets Maria. Could she be the one? Rodgers and Edwards were invited to supply music, but not the incidental themes, which were mostly supplied by Johnny Mandel. The five new songs were recorded in the spring of 1982, likely at Power Station, New York. Who plays on the tracks is hard to discern from the credits, which are unspecific and include the three older songs, too. Only the personnel on 'Tavern On The Green' are known for sure.

Atlantic weren't interested in the soundtrack album, but it was picked up by their former President, Jerry Greenberg. He had left the label (albeit still working for them as a consultant) and had set up Mirage Music with his brother Bob.

Teddy Pendergrass appears in the film performing 'Dream Girl' as the singer in the nightclub scene, which also features Chic at one point. The best of the new songs, 'Why', amazingly, wasn't actually featured in the film!

The soundtrack album features: 'Soup For One' (Chic), 'Why' (Carly Simon), 'Dream Girl' (Teddy Pendergrass), 'I Work For A Livin'' (Fonzi Thornton), 'I Want Your Love' (Chic), 'Let's Go On Vacation' (Sister Sledge), 'Tavern On The Green' (Chic) and 'Jump, Jump' (Debbie Harry). The five new songs are discussed below:

'Soup For One'

Rodgers said that this track is one of his favourites in the *Very Best Of Chic* CD notes (2000). It has a reserved, soulful feel that impresses musically, but the lyrics do an overly good job of relating a humdrum life. It all feels too downbeat for me. Edwards' low-key verse vocal does nothing to dispel that. The song picks up on the chorus when the backing vocals come in for the high harmonies, and the bridge section is a good groove based on the main melody with tasty licks from Rodgers.

There is a 7:57 extended version in the *Savoir Faire* box, which is better because the instrumental sections are allowed to stretch out. Rodgers is the main beneficiary here with extra lead fills, but Sabino is also allowed more room to shine. The only other person on the track is Thompson, who keeps it simple, while Edwards' bass weaves around the melody. There is also an edited 4:00 instrumental version with extra congas and lead guitar that gives it all much more zip. This would have made a better backing track to the album/single version.

The song got a new lease of life when it was sampled by Modjo for their 2000 hit 'Lady (Hear Me Tonight)'. Rodgers later added the song to Chic setlists circa 2013 as a medley with 'Lady'! It still wasn't great, but it did work better with Kimberly Davis and Folami on vocals.

'Why'

This is one of the best songs Chic created with another artist. It was a stylistic change for Carly Simon, as she was best known for her ballads and soft rock output. A full album by her with the Chic Organisation could have been a real tour de force but, sadly, this beauty is all we got. There are strong hints of reggae in the groove, and the combination of that and Simon's yearning, ice-cool, yet also passionate, voice is delicious. Edwards' supple basslines immediately grab your attention, and even the pedestrian drum machine can't cast a cloud over this brilliance.

There are at least two keyboard parts in the mix, weaving together and covering the strings. Rodgers, meanwhile, goes for a staccato pulse riff that stands right out in the mix. Simon's 'lah-di-dah' refrain gives things an 'off-hand' edge to her sangfroid vocals, and there's a nice section (4:02 on the long version) where the backing vocalists take over for a repeated chorus.

The definitive version is the 8:12 remix (on the *Chic Organisation* set). The song was released as a single, and while it stalled at number 74 on the American *Billboard* chart, it really caught on big-time across Europe. It reached number ten in the UK, but there was little association made at the time as to who wrote and played on it, even though the B-side was credited to Chic alone (because it is an instrumental take). The song resurfaced in 1989 when it became a playlist regular in Ibiza's clubs, becoming a key song in what was called the 'Balearic Beat'.

'Dream Girl'

The combination of Chic and former Harold Melvin & The Blue Notes singer Teddy Pendergrass seemed like a perfect match, but it just doesn't catch fire. The 'soupy' (excuse the pun) production doesn't help either. Rodgers might have agreed with that because he tried a remix, which emerged, with little improvement, on *Savoir Faire*.

It opens with an appealing cascading piano motif, but soon sinks into a dull rhythmic groove that does nothing for Pendergrass or Chic. Pendergrass's deep voice isn't a good fit over the backing track. It picks up at 2:28 with a sparkling keyboard hook that plays well against his raspy baritone. From then on, the song has a bit more going for it, but it's still pretty much a misfire.

'I Work For A Living'

Reviewed under Fonzi Thornton's *Don't Throw Your Love Away* album.

'Tavern On The Green'

A completely left-field, almost solo piece by Rodgers, performed on at least two guitars playing in harmony. The tune is a naively pretty melody with a very pastoral 'English' feel to it. Sabino adds some chords on the synth, with a woodwind feel, for minor accompaniment. It remains the most unusual piece of work in the Chic catalogue – a quirky oddball delight that was strictly a one-off. It's a lovely piece that reminds me of Jimmy Page's bucolic excursions with Led Zeppelin.

Tongue In Chic (Chic) (1982)

Personnel:
Nile Rodgers: guitar, backing vocals,
Bernard Edwards: bass, backing vocals, lead vocals on 'Hangin'', 'I Feel Your Love Comin' On' and 'Sharing Love'
Tony Thompson: drums, percussion
Alfa Anderson: lead vocals on 'When You Love Someone' and 'Hey Fool', backing vocals
Luci Martin: backing vocals
Fonzi Thornton, Michelle Cobbs, Jocelyn Brown, Dolette McDonald: harmony and backing vocals
Sammy Figueroa: percussion
Ray Jones: keyboards, rap on 'Chic (Everybody Say)'
Rob Sabino: keyboards
Gene Orloff: string arranger and conductor
Robert Aaron: saxophone
Ray Maldonado: trumpet
Marty Celay: additional guitar on 'When You Love Someone'
Produced and arranged by Bernard Edwards and Nile Rodgers at Power Station, New York, in 1982
Release date: 1 November 1982
Label: Atlantic
Highest chart places: UK: did not chart, US: did not chart
Running time: 32:42
All songs by Edwards and Rodgers.

This is a strong album despite the overuse of the Synclavier and drum machines. Thompson wasn't happy with their use, and he wasn't alone. He admitted to *Echoes* in 1985 that 'Bernard didn't want to use drum machines, he wanted to stick to the old formula.' Vocally, the album feels unbalanced. Edwards takes three leads, one more than Anderson, and poor Martin doesn't get any! Even Ray Jones gets a vocal!

The cover image puns on the album title with a tongue-in-cheek (Chic?) image of a female builder (Anderson) and an intrigued male passer-by (Thompson). It's an amusing flip of the usual social image for this scenario. The back cover group shot is really good, with Rodgers standing out from the others in a mustard yellow trench coat! However, it's clear from their faces how time has taken a toll in such a relatively short period.

Chic toured America in support of the album in late 1982. The strings weren't present, but the brass section of Aaron and Maldonado made the tour. Rodgers, when speaking to *Musician* in April 1992, regretted the decision: 'When we toured the last time, we took two horns instead of strings. It was a disaster.' Thornton and Cobbs were there again, too, on backing vocals, along with both Andy Schwartz and Ray Jones on keyboards. After the tour, Jones accepted a gig with Talking Heads. He assumed he would be returning to the Chic payroll afterwards, but they never picked him up again for studio work. Chic never toured again until the Budokan reunion concerts of 1996.

'Hangin''

Down on the streets for some action. Maldonado's trumpet excels in the intro, with finger clicks and a great interchange between Rodgers and Thompson opening things up in a fun way. Rodgers keeps it snappy, taut and tight in the rhythm while Edwards' rock-solid bass anchors it perfectly against the hand-clap sounding drum track. Edwards sings the song effectively enough, with the Chic choir backing him in the choruses. Robert Aaron's sax solo breaks things up before he joins Maldonado, who plays a great harmony part, on the rhythm.

There are plenty of harmony vocals from here to the end of the song, which always work well with Edward's voice. Rodgers takes a solo at 2:56 with a wonderful, almost muted tone to it. He revealed to Gene Santoro of *Downbeat* in September 1985 that he 'did the solo on a D'Angelico, an old-fashioned Maceo (Parker) kind of riff.' He stays close to the melody, taking off into jazzier diversions as he progresses.

John Taylor (Duran Duran) is a big fan of this song. For me, it's good but too repetitive to be a classic. It was released as a single and got to number 64 in Britain.

'I Feel Your Love Comin' On'

This opens with an a cappella chorus that immediately grabs your attention, followed by Thompson powering in, to put it mildly. A solid groove is created by the synth bass and drum machine. It's Edwards again on lead vocals, which seems odd considering that the opening two songs are devoid of the band's best two lead vocalists. The best section is the bridge (2:22), where different melodies fly in and out from Rodgers, Edwards and Sabino, the latter of whom sounds like he is off to join a Kraftwerk tribute band. Edwards, meanwhile, sounds like he is flirting with 'Good Times' around the three-minute mark. There is a real feel of a band trying out new ideas here; it doesn't sound much like Chic at times, but their DNA is still in there.

It's way too long, just shy of seven minutes, but it attracted the attention of Dmitri From Paris, who came up with an extended remix for the *Chic Organisation* set. It improves on the original with more synths, brass and percussion in the mix, but it's still too long.

'When You Love Someone'

A song of two halves. The first half is a fine Anderson vocal ballad in the 'Warm Summer Night' style – her phrasing is just beautiful. Behind her is a relaxing and warm backing track with strings conducted by Gene Orloff, albeit they are too low in the mix. Ray Jones' piano is the perfect, sweet accompaniment here. This is all just terrific, but boldly, after a brief lull, the tempo is up for part two, introduced by Anderson's 'stars come out tonight and shine so very bright'. The band kick in behind her for what is a glorious, life-affirming panoply of delight.

'Chic (Everybody Say)'

This is a vibrant, cheerful track, complete with overdubbed appreciative crowd noise. The self-mythology strikes similar territory to 'Chic Cheer', but we didn't really need another slice of it. Ray Jones raps about the glories of Chic – interesting that it wasn't Rodgers or Edwards – and he makes a good job of it. The better news is the strings are back, which fits with the song's subject matter, and from 3:06, you get some dizzying lines from them. It peaks when Rodgers joins in with the strings at 3:40, playing a grandstanding rock guitar solo to finish the song.

'Hey Fool'

Anderson's big showcase on the album is a sweetly exquisite song full of simple joy in the music and lyrics. There is no breakdown, and there is little variety in the backing track, but keeping it simple is enough on this occasion. Only Edwards' great swing rhythm in his playing really stands out. It is, in spite of the lack of musical diversions, one of the most typical Chic songs on the album, a lot of that because of Anderson's superb vocal. The fade-out outro is flawed; it fades away without any sense of ending. Despite that, it's an underrated song.

'Sharing Love'

Just 2:40 of this laid-back, almost AOR track showcases Edwards on vocals again. It's not his best vocal in the verses; he pretty much speaks the lyrics, and they would have been better sung by Anderson or Martin. They join in with him in the chorus – the difference is like night and day. The song then comes alive, with a slow-burning, easy, pleasant feel to it.

'City Lights'

They end with this workout that features some great jazzy guitar licks. It plays out really like an instrumental, but there are ensemble harmony lead vocals with a basic set of lyrics that are more like random phrases. It's an ebullient piece and a real 'up' finish to the record. At 1:45 comes a terrific section where Rodgers and Sabino, plus Thompson's cymbals, cue up Edwards' mean, funky bass solo augmented by the plucked strings. Up next is Sabino's piano solo backed by the vocals, with Rodgers harmonising. It's a magical interplay and makes for a wonderful end to the album. This has a heart and soul to it that should have been the template for the album.

Adventures In The Land Of The Good Groove
(Nile Rodgers) (1983)

Personnel:
Nile Rodgers: lead and backing vocals, guitar, drums, keyboards
Bernard Edwards: bass, backing vocals
Tony Thompson: additional drums
Rob Sabino: keyboards
Ray Jones: piano, keyboards
Carmine Rojas, Curtis King, David Spinner, Eddie Martinez, Fonzi Thornton, Frank Simms, George Simms, John Wright, Kenny Williams, Phillip Balou, Rachel Sweet: backing vocals
Sarah Dash: lead vocals on 'My Love Song For You'
Jeremy Steele: pedal steel guitar
Produced and arranged by Nile Rodgers at Power Station, New York, in 1982
Release date: 11 March 1983
Label: Mirage
Highest chart places: UK: did not chart, US: did not chart
Running time: 41:39
All songs by Nile Rodgers.

Rodgers signed to Mirage for a solo deal, but this album fell short of expectations. The title was good and promised a lot, so it was disappointing to get an album that was so limited in its range.

The record's focus on electronics via synths and syndrums makes for a technical, impersonal album lacking in warmth. Even the contributions of his many Chic comrades can't lift it. The core band is Chic, and most of the vocalists are Chic alumni.

The record, which impressed David Bowie, did not take off and become a commercial success. One specific problem is Rodgers' lead vocals, which are, at best, adequate. Rodgers said in *Le Freak:* 'I knew it was a flop right away. I'd been so afraid of being labelled a disco musician that I was too tentative about the album's direction. And the songs weren't hooky enough.'

The packaging didn't help sell it either, the cover being an obscure 17th-century map of Lower Manhattan, thus the land of the good groove! The 2008 remaster added extended versions of the title track and 'Yum Yum', which, sadly, in this instance, proved the old adage that less is more.

'The Land Of The Good Groove'

The intro is interesting with wide panned percussion and Rodgers' guitar groove fixed in the centre of the spectrum. It's his guitar that defines the track, living up to the title's promise. The song itself never really takes off, though, and doesn't quite come to fruition. The poor lyrics are a giveaway that this was a work still in progress.

'Yum-Yum'

This is firmly about sex. Nowhere else in the Chic canon do they touch on the subject so overtly. The rhythm track of synth, guitar and drum machine anticipates where Rodgers was going sonically with Madonna. The high notes of the keyboard melody and Rodgers' chugging rhythm are pleasing. Sadly, it's let down by the dreadful lyrics and Rodgers' strident delivery.

'Beet'

This has a more organic feel to it. Edwards' bass adds welcome strength and melody and it sounds like Thompson on drums rather than a machine. However, this is still a long way from top-drawer material. Rodgers delivers some scorching guitar licks over a bubbly synth in the bridge section, which works well, before swapping to a rhythmic, twanging blues groove which brings to mind the kind of feel Stevie Ray Vaughan adds to *Let's Dance.*

'Get Her Crazy'

It's drum machines and synths all over the big intro, with Rodgers playing the guitar hook. The chest-beating, doubled or trebled roar by Rodgers of the title is immediately followed by the more plaintive solo vocals of affirmation and intent. His voice is not usually a strong point, but it is more effective here. It all helps push this song up to being one of the best on the album. It has an urgency and feel to it that has been lacking until now.

His rhythm playing is vintage Rodgers, but when he is faded up at 2:39 for the instrumental break, it's simply fabulous. His guitars (two rhythm parts and at least one lead) are right up front and central in the mix, and it's the first shining moment on the album. He maintains this level to the end. What is missing is the extra rhythmic groove Edwards could have supplied and a Chic-style keyboard part from Sabino, etc., but this is as good as it gets without that.

'It's All In Your Hands'

This has a restrained feel to it, which would be even better without the drum machine pattern that crashes all over it. In fact, an overall more thoughtful musical backing to Rodgers' chiming guitar lines would have elevated this song.

'Rock Bottom'

There's a brooding but bubbly feel to this deep groove, as suits the title. It highlights the difference Edwards makes when he is fully in tandem and involved in a song. It's the best example on the album of the two men playing in sync with each other, and it benefits from Thompson playing the drums too. You have to love the rhythm track breakdown section, but the highlight is Rodgers' stunning guitar solo (3:21), which is a real beast of a sound rooted in blues scales. It is one of the best solos he has ever played on record and I wish it was longer. It's that good. The effect is heightened by Rodgers' tight rhythm part continuing in the background. This song is an unexpected Chic-style wonder.

'My Love Song For You'

An equal best with 'Rock Bottom' is this classic Chic-style ballad. Fortunately, Rodgers saw fit to bring in Labelle's Sarah Dash to duet with him. She must have inspired Rodgers as he turns in his best vocal on the album. While it's excellent, even including those Chic-style piano and keyboard melodies courtesy of Ray Jones, you can't help but wonder how Alfa Anderson or Luci Martin would have handled it. Overall, this is an excellent track that deserves more attention.

'Most Down'

Unfortunately, the album closes with this inconsequential song replete with uninteresting electronic rhythms. Rodgers uses a vocoder at times, which only adds to the automated feel. His almost whispered verse vocals and his trusty rhythm guitar are the best things about the song.

Glad To Be Here (Bernard Edwards) (1983)

Personnel:
Bernard Edwards: lead vocals, bass
Nile Rodgers: guitar
Tony Thompson: drums on 'Glad To Be Here'
Rob Sabino: keyboards
Eddie Martinez: lead guitar
Sammy Figueroa: percussion on 'Hard Loving Man'
Jocelyn Brown: lead vocals on 'Don't Do Me Wrong'
Ray Chew: mini-moog synthesiser, piano
Ed Walsh: synthesiser, vocoder
Jeff Mironov: guitar
Yogi Horton: drums on all but ''Your Love Is Good To Me' and 'Glad To Be Here'
Georg Wadenius: guitar on 'You Don't Know Me'
Alfa Anderson, Luci Martin, Luther Vandross, Michelle Cobbs, Dolette McDonald, B.J. Nelson, Curtis King, Jocelyn Brown, Yvonne Lewis, Phillip Ballou: backing vocals
Lenny Pickett: saxophone on 'You Really Got A Hold On Me'
Produced by Bernard Edwards at Power Station, New York, in 1983
Release date: 1983
Label: Atlantic
Highest chart places: UK: did not chart, US: did not chart
Running time: 33:00
All songs by Bernard Edwards, except as noted.

Edwards' album is full of Chic personnel. The trick here, then, was to make the album sound like a solo album rather than a Chic album. It's something he manages to pull off, helped by singing all the lead parts himself, which ensures the songs are all in his comfortable range.

It's a better listen than Rodgers' *Adventures* because the songs are generally stronger and the sound is more band-based. You also can't underestimate the power of that formidable lineup of backing vocalists. Although Rodgers plays on the album, the heavy lifting was by old friend Eddie Martinez, so the 'Chicness' is downplayed by the reduction of Rodgers' guitar. Despite this, the album sounds exactly as you might expect – no strings and little brass – but these are all tunes that could have been on a late-period Chic album. Sammy Figueroa plays on just one track, but his underwhelming opinion of the album is that 'it wasn't incredible, but it was good.'

The colourful front cover, which focuses on Edwards' bass as the 'star', is eyecatching. The man himself adopts a typically humble pose on the back cover.

'Your Love Is Good To Me'

This track opens with a combination of crunching synths from Ray Chew over a Linn drum machine programmed by Chew and Edwards. Oddly, Edwards decided to open his only solo album with a track with no bass! So the focus is on his voice, and interestingly, the riffing rhythm guitar by Rodgers. The verses highlight Edwards' vocals as he sings alone, and he acquits himself well within his limited range. For the choruses, he is joined by the backing vocals, which are tremendous, really pushing the chorus home. While Edwards goes for a similar approach to Rodgers in terms of utilising technology, it comes over as more organic here because of the strong vocal arrangement and that rumbling, funky mini-moog part from Ray Chew. Overall, this is a fine track.

'Don't Do Me Wrong'
This one is in the same vein as the great Chic ballads. Jocelyn Brown sings effective lead vocals, with Anderson and Martin on background vocals, on this tender song with sensitive instrumentation. Edwards' expressive bass part is central here; the song revolves around his playing without him ever being overly forceful. It's a masterful piece of playing, and credit must go to Rodgers for his subtle 'ticking' rhythm part and exquisite solo.

'You Don't Know Me'
This brief, sultry song sees Edwards outlining his position in a relationship. Cleverly, Edwards takes the verses, while some of the backing vocalists take the chorus, giving the impression that, despite his words, they are still unimpressed with his actions. The instrumentation is basic, with the melody carried by a Fender Rhodes, and also the superb bass playing of the main man. It's a good song, but very short at a mere 2:32 long. If it had been developed more, say with at least a strong bridge section, it would have helped. One instant improvement would have been to have just one female singer in the chorus in order to highlight the personal nature of the track.

'Joy Of Life'
This track is built around Edwards' funky bassline. When Rodgers' guitar joins in and plays the contrasting licks, it makes for a definitive Chic groove. The Chic vocal choir are showcased in the choruses with Edwards faded right down. He doesn't have to stretch himself in the verses too much, which he sings alone. For what it is, it's a good enough song, but there's nothing distinctive about it to make it pop. The best part of it is the Chic choir, who give the song all of its dynamics.

'You've Really Got A Hold On Me' (Smokey Robinson)
Edwards doesn't get near to the playful longing of the original version by Smokey Robinson & The Miracles, but this is a warm, lovely effort. The big switch here is that he sings it as a duet. Jocelyn Brown partners with Edwards in a lovely arrangement by Luther Vandross, which is a real treat. The pair are great together as 'both parties' sound wrapped up in each other.

The sax solo by Lenny Pickett is extraordinary – a wailing, squealing solo that is a huge contrast to the restraint and taut feel of the song. A smoother solo might have worked better for the song, but you can't deny that it has impact. All in all, this is one of the best songs on the album and stands up to repeated listens.

'Hard Loving Man'

Edwards ups the groove factor with a welcome wandering bass run in the verses. The drums are augmented by the always special Sammy Figueroa on percussion. Again, Edwards makes intelligent use of the vocal choir to give him support on the choruses, so you get the sweeter complementary backing tones to his deep lead vocal. Eddie Martinez handles all the guitars, including the 'rock guitar' solo, which isn't an easy fit for the song. It's still good in spite of that.

'Glad To Be Here'

Finishing off as we started the album, a more synthy 1980s sound dominates the intro and Ed Walsh tries his hand on the vocoder. However, that intro gives way to the biggest groove on the album, featuring Rodgers on guitar (alongside Martinez) and Tony Thompson on drums. Edwards is impeccable on the bass, and it is probably his best work on the album. It really is a masterclass from him in how to drive a song along on the bass. The runs, fills and licks he plays are vintage Edwards. The instrumental section from 2:48 is where it all gets seriously funky with the bass notes from the synth blending with Edwards' bass.

Vocally, there's not much to it; it's a nursery rhyme type lyric with little to say, but somehow it works if you don't take much notice of the words! Musically, though, this track is a great way to finish off the album and leaves you wanting more.

Let's Dance (David Bowie) (1983)

Personnel:
David Bowie: lead vocals
Nile Rodgers: guitar
Bernard Edwards: bass on 'Without You'
Tony Thompson: drums on 'Cat People', 'Without You'
Omar Hakim: drums
Rob Sabino: keyboards
Sammy Figueroa: percussion
Frank Simms, George Simms, David Spinner: backing vocals
Stevie Ray Vaughan: lead guitar
Carmine Rojas: bass
Robert Aaron: tenor saxophone
Stan Harrison: tenor saxophone, flute
Steve Elson: baritone saxophone, flute
Mac Gollehon: trumpet
Produced and arranged by David Bowie & Nile Rodgers at Power Station, New York, in December 1982
Release date: 14 April 1983
Label: EMI
Highest chart places: UK: 1, US: 4
Running time: 39:41
All songs by David Bowie, except as noted.

Bowie left RCA in 1982 but didn't immediately sign a new deal with another company. It meant he could make the album he wanted to make and then shop it around. It's unlikely that RCA ever had any serious words about his output with them, in spite of his diversity and genre hopping. For the most part, he had a fan base that accepted and welcomed that, and his records sold very well. What Bowie was heading towards now, what he wanted, was his biggest record yet.

It was to be a new album for a new era. He had apparently enthused over the album *One Down* by Material. Nile Rodgers' guitar contributions on two tracks, along with his track record of making hit albums, further convinced Bowie that this was a man he could work with and wasn't afraid to branch out into other styles and genres. A meeting between the two at The Continental Hotel in New York sealed the deal. Rodgers modestly opined to *Musician* in 1983: 'David could've had any producer, white or black, he wanted. He could have gone with Quincy Jones and had a more sure-fire chance at a hit. But he called me up, and for that I feel honoured.'

The initial demos were recorded at Bowie's home in Lausanne, Switzerland. Working with Nile meant a different tone to the album, but then Bowie had always been a musical chameleon. Equally significant was who took part in the sessions. Logically, you would have expected reasonably long-term associates like Carlos Alomar (guitar), Dennis Davis (drums) and George Murray (bass) to be present, but none of them are, although Alomar did make the *Serious Moonlight* tour following the album. Instead, a new core band was put together by Rodgers, and the bulk of it included Chic alumni. Sammy Figueroa returned on percussion, and Rob Sabino came in on keyboards/synths, but there were changes in the rhythm section. Rodgers had doubts about calling in Thompson and Edwards because of their potential unreliability due to drug issues. Because the record was such a key album for Bowie, he opted to call in Omar Hakim (drums) and Carmine Rojas (bass) instead. In the end, Thompson came in for three songs (one still uncertain) and Edwards just one. Figueroa appears for the last time on percussion with Rodgers and/or Edwards. He wasn't upset by the parting of ways, saying, 'They gave me my name. Even though I was already doing a bunch of stuff in New York with so many other people, it was really Nile and Bernard who put my name out there big.'

Some have criticised the album for veering too much towards a pop/jazzy vibe. But Rodgers asserted to the *Washington Post* in 2016: 'Bowie and I both loved jazz. Everybody he mentioned, I knew, and everybody I mentioned, he knew. So I knew I could put the jazzy side of Chic on his music. The day I changed his song 'Let's Dance' to a jazzier vibe, I said, 'David, have I made this record too funky?' 'Nile darling', he said, 'is there such a thing as too funky?"

Bowie booked Power Station for three weeks to record the album, which Rodgers felt was partly to see how things worked out. Fortunately, everything went swimmingly, with Rodgers fostering a great atmosphere of camaraderie with the musicians. Late arrival Thompson was impressed by Bowie, as he attested to *One Two Testing* in 1985: 'The thing with that album was that, for the first time, I was recording in the studio at the same time as the singer. He was only putting on a reference vocal, but it was great; we had this eye contact. If he hadn't been singing, I would have thought, 'a fill should go about here'. But watching him, I tried in different places, and they worked.' Bowie stuck with the reference tracks, recording his final vocal *and* keeping Thompson's fills in place.

Stan Harrison (sax/flute) was one of the brass section. He recalls:

Let's Dance is the first record I did with Nile. The first song we recorded was 'Ricochet', which is still one of my favourites. The horn section was overdubbed, and we played on most, but not all, of the songs. Keep in mind that Mac Gollehon is also playing trumpet on this record. These sessions were extremely happy ones. It's hard to describe how intoxicating it was to meet and record with David Bowie and Nile Rodgers, all on the same day. It was otherworldly. A truly amazing, awe-inspiring experience. Nile couldn't have done a better job of making us all feel comfortable. We all felt free to contribute and, in fact, we did. He listened to every idea we had. Some were used, some were not. But he listened. David was the same way. There was no pressure, only joy.

Bowie's only contribution on the personnel front was bringing in Stevie Ray Vaughan. Vaughan had finished recording his debut album, *Texas Flood,* less than a month before the *Let's Dance* sessions commenced. Bowie's awareness of him as the 'right' lead guitarist for the project was based on seeing him perform at the Montreux Jazz Festival on 17 July 1982. One performance was all it took to convince him. Rodgers was less sure at first, feeling there was little more to him than an Albert King-style blues player. Vaughan's playing soon won him over, and he ended up recording overdubs on six of the eight tracks. His playing, on a Fender Stratocaster, is superb, adding much character. They finished the album within 17 days, according to Rodgers in *Le Freak*, with Bowie and Vaughan completing all their parts in just two days.

The album sequencing is interesting. Side one opens with the three big-hitter singles in a row, and ends with the superb 'Without You' – the biggest 'Chic' number on the album. 'Let's Dance' feels like it's in the wrong place – for me, it should be track one. Side two is weak by comparison, with little standing up to the quality of side one. It comes over as a mixed bag of styles, including a remake ('Cat People'), a cover version (the admittedly inspired 'Criminal World') and two weak new Bowie songs – 'Ricochet' and 'Shake It'. The fact that he included two remakes and the cover suggests that he was short on new, top-quality material of his own.

EMI were the lucky company to get the album. They gave Bowie a five-year contract for five albums for a $10 million payout. As Bowie and Rodgers hoped, and EMI expected, the public lapped up the album and the singles from it. The 'Let's Dance' single was released in March to a great reception from fans and media alike (number one in Britain and America), with the album following in April. EMI must have been delighted at the sales, which saw Bowie picking up countless casual buyers, but nothing he did for them after it got as close to hitting the same sweet spot sales-wise. Rodgers watched the media buzz over what became, and remains, Bowie's biggest-selling album. He noted that his contribution as producer/band leader/arranger seemed to get passed over in the noise. Bowie later conceded in 1993 on the *Black Tie, White Noise* film that *Let's Dance* was 'Nile's vision of what my music should sound like, and I'd provided the songs.'

The ensuing tour was a huge success, but Vaughan didn't go out with Bowie. He dropped out at the last minute following prolonged disagreements with Bowie's management. Thompson did the tour, as he outlined to *International Musician & Recording World* in October 1985: 'I hadn't been on the road for a while, so I was itching to get back. I had just finished up my parts on *Let's Dance* and was hanging around the studio when I overheard David talking to some people about doing a tour. So, I told him, 'Hey, if you're looking for a drummer."

'Modern Love'
Rodgers opens the album with his 6/8 scratchy hook, followed by Hakim coming in with startlingly loud drums. It's just the two of them until the melody and the first verse come in. Lyrically, it's streamlined, almost there purely to accompany the surging riffs and rhythm. Bowie delivers the lyrics effortlessly well and is especially convincing on the sly opening couplet: 'I know when to go out, and when to stay in, get things done'. There are two excellent sax solos, of which Stan Harrison notes that 'the sax solo in the middle is a baritone solo played by Steve Elson. The solo at the end is a tenor solo played by Robert Aaron.'

All in all, it's a dynamic opening shot and a very good song. It was the third single from the album, hitting number two in the UK and number 14 in America.

'China Girl' (Bowie/Iggy Pop)
This song originally appeared on Iggy Pop's album *The Idiot*. What Bowie's intentions were in regard to a new interpretation or arrangement were not disclosed to Rodgers. Bowie merely played it to him as a song he thought could be a hit. Rodgers wasn't so keen on it but came up with a rearrangement showcasing what, in *Le Freak*, he called 'a catchy, Asian-sounding riff'. Bowie loved Rodgers' work and they recorded it there and then.

The bulk of the guitar – the 'Asian' parts – are all by Rodgers. While there is an almost languid feel to his playing, it's in direct contrast to the clipped, pumping bass and Omar Hakim's drums. Bowie croons the lyrics, effectively straddling Rodgers' parts and Sabino's keyboard block chords. It's a real triumph for Bowie, who gives the lyrics full measure, most memorably on the 'ssshhhh' and 'oh baby, just you shut your mouth'. Vaughan is used sparingly but effectively. He plays the first tasteful, bluesy solo at 3:27 before returning thereafter for another solo (4:32), which is effectively more of the same. The option was not taken to let him burn over the outro, which is Bowie fading into the distance on a chorus with Rodgers' 'Asian' lick on repeat.

The song fails to fully resonate with me, but it has those little moments of magic in the vocal melodies, as noted. It was the second single from the album and reached number two in the UK and number ten in America.

'Let's Dance'
This was the first song recorded for the sessions, with Rodgers picking it out as the one to set the tone. It evolved from a folky-style, acoustic guitar-based demo, which Bowie put together in Switzerland. Rodgers then got his hands on it and came up with the familiar arrangement. The intro is a fabulous tip of the hat to 'Twist And Shout' (as performed by The Isley Brothers and The Beatles), and from there to the end, it's a beautiful, joyous piece of work that cuts loose for the dance floor. Bowie had been exuberant on record before, but he excels here.

Hakim holds the rock-steady drumbeat, with Figueroa adding congas and even getting his own chance to shine in the breakdown section at 5:03. When the brass come in at 5:36, it initially reminds me of the brass from 'I Want Your Love', until they take off for a maelstrom of the brass section improvising and bouncing off each other. Stan Harrison comments that 'the back-and-forth sax soloing is between Steve (Elson) on baritone and yours truly on tenor.'

Figueroa expands on his percussion part:

> That tune is all about the voice and the percussion. I said, 'Do you want anything in particular, David?', and he said, 'No, you play whatever you want and when I come back, I will listen to it.' So he went to lunch for two and a half hours. Bob Clearmountain (engineer) said to me, 'Play your heart out and play the sounds you think fit this tune.' I played some cowbells and woodblocks and then the congas came in way later for the dance part. All of that percussion was done in one take, and Bob said, 'That's it, Sammy, no more, that stays.' When David came back, Bob said to him, 'You want to rest a little?', and he said, 'Yeah, I'm gonna lay out.' He took a nap for about 25 minutes and he got up and he said, 'Alright, let's give it a go!' He listened to it and he was really quiet. Nobody said anything and I was thinking, 'Oh boy, I hope he likes it.' He still didn't say a word for about five minutes, and then he looks at me and he goes, 'Brilliant!' I said, 'Holy shit, thank God!' He said, 'Leave it alone, make it louder, that's it.'

The guitar parts are an equally impressive feature of the song. Vaughan adds superb colour with his licks, showing exactly why Bowie wanted him on the sessions. His playing has such sensitivity and he is the perfect foil for Bowie's voice.

It's a great song and the public loved it, too, sending it to number one on both sides of the Atlantic. The single version is three-and-a-half minutes shorter, and different (shorter) solos were used from the album version because of this. Either version is great, but the go-to version is the album one.

'Without You'

As the style of this is very Chic, it arguably sounds almost like Bowie is putting in a guest vocal on his own album! The presence of Edwards on bass, alongside Thompson on drums, increases the Chic quotient, which is also enhanced by a low-key Bowie vocal and an understated performance from Vaughan. Edwards was called in to play on the track because, as Rodgers said in *Le Freak,* it was a 'tricky bass line' and Rojas had struggled with it. Edwards, however, nailed it in just 13 minutes and one run-through! He gives the song its swing feel, contrasting with Thompson's jerky drum pattern.

It's an overlooked song on the album, and perhaps its calm, almost tranquil feel, coming after the big three on side one, is partly why it hasn't gathered more plaudits. But this is a remarkable vocal from Bowie, and while it is a really heartfelt performance, there is also a distance to his delivery, enhanced by the muted musical backdrop.

Rodgers handles the sparkly rhythm guitar part, while Vaughan adds the sensitive blues licks, which wrap around Rodgers' guitar. Vaughan can mostly be heard in the long outro. It's a gorgeous piece of work all round. In November 1983, it was released as a single in America (where it reached number 73), Japan, the Netherlands and Spain.

'Ricochet'

Originally titled 'Shame, Shame (It's Not The End Of The World)', this is the most experimental track. It has an expansive sound, which Rodgers described as 'Afrobeat', with Figueroa's percussion to the fore alongside powerhouse drumming from Hakim or Thompson. Quite why Bowie adopts a Welsh accent for the spoken word sections, on which he outlines industrial trials and tribulations, is a mystery.

Musically, it's a confused jumble of sound and Bowie sounds like he is singing a different track to the musicians. He was never happy with the final track, telling *Musician* in 1987: 'It didn't roll the way it should have, the syncopation was wrong. It had an ungainly gait; it should have flowed. I want to do that on the tour, but playing the beat the right way. Nile did his own thing to it, but it wasn't quite what I'd had in mind when I wrote the thing.' It never made it to the regular setlist on the *Serious Moonlight* tour, if it was ever played at all. It is also the only song on the album not to have featured somewhere on a single.

'Criminal World' (Peter Godwin/Duncan Browne/Sean Lyons/Bowie)

The original song was released by Metro as a single in 1977, but it was banned from airplay on the BBC due to the sexual nature of the lyrics. Those lyrics were 'adapted' by Bowie (who also completely re-wrote the second verse) for his own version.

The Metro song is taken at a slower tempo and misses Rodgers' ringing guitar riff. Credit to Bowie and Rodgers because their reworking of the song is clever and effective. It is subdued in its feel, however, with only Vaughan's solo breaking loose with some fire to it. It's probably the best song on side two, but still a world away from the rich delights on offer on side one.

'Cat People (Putting Out Fire)' (Bowie/Giorgio Moroder)

This is a re-recording of the song Bowie put out as a single a year earlier from the *Cat People* movie soundtrack. It's a very different interpretation, with more urgency and power than the original take. Bowie's vocal sets the bar high with a passionate, strong vocal. Then there are Vaughan's memorable, fiery solos. At the heart of it all is Tony Thompson on drums, making, it is often said, the second of his three appearances on the album. He is just excellent, giving the song real power and ferocity. Plaudits also to Sammy

Figueroa on congas, whose part adds a lot of character to the percussion track, if you can tune your brain to hear him, as he is way too low in the mix. There was apparently an unspecified problem late on with Rojas's bass part, which had to be fixed. On this occasion, it didn't warrant a call to Edwards to come in and redo the part.

Because it was a relatively recent (at the time) re-recording, it wasn't received perhaps as well as it deserved, overshadowed by the original single.

'Shake It'

An odd end to the album, this feels like a B-side track at best. There is a part where it comes to life at 1:39 when the backing vocals support Bowie's cry with 'What's my line?' This section is repeated later and similarly increases interest. Vaughan's shards of guitar add bright touches, but otherwise, this is a forgettable throwaway song that doesn't deserve to be on the record.

Believer (Chic) (1983)

Personnel:
Nile Rodgers: guitar, backing vocals, lead vocals/rap on 'Party Everybody'
Bernard Edwards: bass, backing vocals
Tony Thompson: drums, percussion
Rob Sabino: keyboards, piano
Alfa Anderson: lead vocals on 'Believer', 'You Are Beautiful', 'Give Me The Lovin'', 'Show Me Your Light' and 'In Love With The Music', backing vocals
Luci Martin: lead vocals on 'Believer', 'You Are Beautiful', 'Take A Closer Look' and 'Show Me Your Light', backing vocals
Fonzi Thornton, Curtis King, Brenda White: harmony and backing vocals
Produced and arranged by Bernard Edwards and Nile Rodgers at Power Station, New York, in 1983
Release date: 14 November 1983 Label: Atlantic
Highest chart places: UK: did not chart, US: did not chart
Running time: 37:42
All songs by Edwards and Rodgers.

Chic were by now disintegrating as the Rodgers and Edwards partnership fell apart, allegedly exacerbated by issues with drugs. But there was also the intense work rate they had put themselves under, as well as Rodgers' solo success producing and playing with Bowie. This final album featured all the music played by a tightly focused core of four: Rodgers, Edwards, Thompson and Sabino. The only issue is the clash between the traditional Chic style and the introduction of synth keyboards and programmed drums. It often gives the album a clinical feel that doesn't sit well. The strings and brass are missed, too. Yet, there is still plenty to enjoy.

The cover, designed by the Japanese designer and illustrator Pater Sato, doesn't help sell the album. We get five portraits in mixed media, but they're all curiously flat-looking and sketchy. The five don't look their best either, with Rodgers, in particular, looking sombre. The new Chic logo works, though – a colourful, very 1980s, bright touch.

Commercially, the album bombed – it didn't chart at all in America or Britain, which is a real shame because the last Chic album deserved better than that. The single, 'Give Me The Lovin'', also didn't chart in America and wasn't even released in Britain.

With the album over, Chic effectively ceased as a named entity, with their final music together coming for Madonna's *Like A Virgin*. In spite of hopes from Edwards and Thompson of cutting another record, it wouldn't be until 1992 that the 'brand' was brought back for *Chic-Ism*.

'Believer'

An excellent start to the album, Edwards' propulsive bass work helps offset the crashing drums, which needed to be dialled down. Rodgers is forceful in the chorus, while Anderson is clipped and ice-cool in the verses. The verses are more interesting, with great licks and phrases from Rodgers, while Anderson, Martin and the backing vocalists channel early Chic (as in 'My Forbidden Lover') in style. The bridge foregoes the Chic breakdown, with Anderson riffing on the title while the band play a tasteful variation on the main melody, with some lovely guitar figures from Rodgers. It's excellent stuff. The second half of the song (from 2:41), likewise, is better, with increased urgency and some excellent line swapping between the core vocalists (Anderson, Martin and Thornton, at least) while Rodgers' guitar swirls from speaker to speaker. Heady stuff, indeed!

'You Are Beautiful'

Rodgers' nagging, insistent guitar line is pure Chic gold. It opens with a vocoder (Rodgers, maybe), and from there, it's classic Chic. Cheekily, the lyrics reference Clark Gable's 'Frankly my dear, I don't give a damn' from *Gone With The Wind*. The impersonation is spot-on and takes you right back to the 'yowsah, yowsah, yowsah' from 'Dance, Dance, Dance'. Sabino's synths are superb walls of sound that call to mind his work with Madonna. They work so well in the context of this song. Edwards gets in a killer lick at the end of each phrase that keeps things moving along. It's nice, too, to hear Tony Thompson getting a chance to stretch out more on the drums than he usually does. He really makes his presence felt with a driving display of power and technique.

'Take A Closer Look'

Time for a solo lead vocal from Martin and this strong ballad shows off her lush, rich voice. It's similar in feel to 'I Loved You More' with a more upbeat feel in the chorus. It's such a strong song that it would have worked equally as well with just Martin alone and Sabino's sublime piano part. My only quibble with the song is Thompson's big drums, giving it a power it doesn't require. None of the other musicians match him in intensity. Rodgers is the one who might have matched him and thrown in a rock guitar-style solo, but he doesn't. Instead, he is quite subtle and only really noticeable in the outro, where he throws in a few little licks.

'Give Me The Lovin''

There's a strong spirit and feel here that is enthralling. The drum part is too strident and overcooked, but even so, it can't affect the sheer power and guts of the vocals. It's an ensemble lead vocal for the big, catchy chorus, which is a nice contrast to Alfa's scene-setting explanatory verses. Maybe it's a bit repetitive, but it carries me along with it just fine. The song breaks new, exciting ground at 2:40, where it changes rhythm with Rodgers playing a catchy, loopy new riff. After that, there's a long outro of Alfa singing call-and-response with the backing vocalists. They could have kept going on that for ages, as far as I am concerned, but it drops down to a killer a cappella fadeout. It was released as a single in America and Spain.

'Show Me Your Light'
This track showcases a great harmony lead vocal arrangement by Anderson and Martin, along with the vocoder from possibly Rodgers. The vocals have an airy breeziness to them, which gives the song the light feel suiting the title. I could have done without the vocoder, but that's the only major flaw. On a less annoying level of criticism, the electro rhythms and sonic pulse beat are a bit too ice-cool for the groove. It needed a more organic instrumental backing track and this one would have really taken off and flown.

'You Got Some Love For Me'
This is a very poppy song, which is limited in the first half by the uninteresting synth drum pattern. There is some gorgeous lead guitar from Rodgers, which shines, plus dazzling piano from Sabino. At 2:27, the drums drop back in the mix a little and Edwards leads the way into a delightful, jazzy extended ending with Rodgers trading lines with Sabino. That second half is terrific.

'In Love With Music'
This is a really feel-good, happy tune. Anderson is terrific, showcasing some old-school Chic vocals. She sounds energised and uses her range to maximum effect to get every nuance across. The backing track also firmly nods to past glories in the appealing chord structure: Gmin7, Cmin7, Dmin7, Fmin7. It never pops out at you, but it is the perfect backing. It leaves Anderson the opportunity to completely own this song.

'Party Everybody'
Right from the off, the drums (hopefully the drum machine and not Thompson) do the song no favours. Then, in comes Rodgers, who raps out the lyrics in what sounds for all the world like an answer to, or part two of, 'Rapper's Delight'. He is obviously enjoying it and having fun, but there is little here to love. Edwards, who is a marvel, is the exception, his parts being plain and simple, decorated with hooky licks and runs that keep you listening. Rodgers nearly redeems himself with an off-kilter guitar solo (at 2:48) that is, at the very least, 'different' for him as he wails and slides away. In the final analysis, this is a poor ending to the album and to Chic.

Outtake
'Just Call Me'
This was first released on the *Savoir Faire* box set, with overdubs added to the original recording by Richard Hilton. What Hilton tellingly adds is a string

synth part that makes you realise how much you have missed the strings on the entire album.

It's a terrific, tight, catchy song, with Martin shining on lead vocals, augmented by the synth strings. It is a much better song, in fact, than most of those on the album, and the only reason it must have been left off is because it's in a similar zone to say 'Believer' and 'Give Me The Lovin''.

Like A Virgin (Madonna) (1984)

Personnel:
Madonna: lead vocals, backing vocals
Nile Rodgers: electric guitar, Synclavier on 'Material Girl' and 'Stay', synth on 'Material Girl', acoustic guitar, string arrangements and string conductor on 'Love Don't Live Here Anymore'
Bernard Edwards: bass on 'Material Girl, 'Like A Virgin', 'Love Don't Live Here Anymore' and 'Shoo-Bee-Doo'
Tony Thompson: drums on 'Material Girl, 'Like A Virgin', 'Love Don't Live Here Anymore' and 'Shoo-Bee-Doo'
Rob Sabino: synth on all except 'Material Girl', Fender Rhodes, piano on 'Shoo-Bee-Doo'
Karen Milne and Kermit Moore: string contractor
Frank Simms, George Simms, Curtis King: backing vocals on all except 'Like A Virgin'
Brenda King: backing vocals on 'Shoo-Bee-Doo'
Lenny Pickett: saxophone solo on 'Shoo-Bee-Doo'
Jimmy Bralower: drum machine programming on all tracks without Tony Thompson
Nathaniel S. Hardy Jnr: keyboards on 'Material Girl' and 'Love Don't Live Here Anymore'
Produced and arranged by Nile Rodgers, Madonna and Stephen Bray at Power Station, New York, between April and September 1984
Release date: 12 November 1984
Label: WEA/Sire
Highest chart places: UK: 1, US: 1
Running time: 38:34
All songs by Madonna and Stephen Bray, except as noted.

Madonna was aiming to build on the slow-burning success of her self-titled debut album, which took a year to reach its peak of number eight in October 1984 on the US album chart. Three of the singles from it – 'Holiday', 'Lucky Star' and 'Borderline' did well in the charts worldwide and helped push the album to the top. It's noticeable that Curtis Hudson (on 'Holiday') and Paul Pesco (on 'Lucky Star') both sound uncannily like Nile Rodgers! Equally, one of the two backing singers on 'Holiday' is former Chic singer Norma Jean Wright.

Madonna's style at this point was focused on dance music tunes with strong melodic hooks and polished arrangements. Stephen Erlwine's 'Madonna Overview' on Allmusic in 2012 claimed with some justification that the album had a 'huge role in popularising dance music as *popular* music again.' She outlined to MTV in 1984 what had attracted her to want to work with Rodgers: 'I think he embodies a lot of different styles that my music embodies. He's very close to the black sound, funk. I mean, the stuff he did with Chic, Sister Sledge and Diana Ross is just phenomenal, but he's also made a lot of great pop records with David Bowie, Duran Duran and INXS.' Another aspect of working with Rodgers was that it would mean working with stellar studio musicians. There's nothing wrong with the playing on her debut, but who can recall the musicians' names?

Rodgers recalled in his autobiography that the first time Madonna played him her demos, she misunderstood his quiet attentiveness as a lack of appreciation. She told him: 'If you don't love all of these songs, we can't work together.' Thinking quickly, he replied, 'Well, to be honest with you, I don't love *all* these songs, but I can promise you this – by the time we're finished with them, I will!' She was impressed and reassured, telling MTV in 1984: 'As soon as we met, we hit it off really well and we thought it would be a great union.'

Rodgers told *Sound On Sound* in April 2005: 'I told her that her first album was brilliant, but it was so electronic and technical that the subliminal artistry of Madonna didn't come through. I thought that if she made a more organic record, even though it was a dance/pop record, people would relate to her artistry in a way that would be astonishing. And she trusted me and went for that.' Rodgers' own recordings in the 1980s (both solo and with Chic) had been prone to sterility with the electronic parts, but here, the blend of the electronic parts and musicians works well, adding dynamics and a range that her debut album lacked.

Three key songs by outside writers were suggested to Madonna by Michael 'Mo' Ostin (Warner's A&R). The two new songs he felt were perfect for the album were 'Material Girl' and 'Like A Virgin'. While Madonna favoured 'Like A Virgin' – and saw it as the album title – Rodgers was more taken with 'Material Girl'. Both made it to the final selection, as did Ostin's other inspired suggestion of a cover version of the iconic Rose Royce song 'Love Don't Live Here Anymore'.

The album was recorded, according to Rodgers, in six weeks and was a relatively simple process. Despite one oft-reported occasion when she berated Edwards for turning up late, it seems Madonna was happy with the recording sessions and was grateful to Rodgers in particular, as she asserted to MTV in 1984: 'We just have a really good chemistry and he understands my musicality. He's a trained musician and I'm not really. I don't know musical terminology; he can just read my mind. He's very sensitive; I think he could work with anyone who's good.'

This was the last major cooperative effort by the Chic Organisation, with Rodgers, Edwards, Thompson and Sabino all together on 'Material Girl, 'Like A Virgin', 'Love Don't Live Here Anymore' and 'Shoo-Bee-Doo'. Thompson saw the writing on the wall, as he made clear to *One Two Testing* in 1985: 'In the end, it got to be too candy-coated and I was really frustrated with the whole thing. Nile was bringing in a lot of drum machines and playing them to death.' The man who was key to that and worked with Rodgers for several years to come was Jimmy Bralower. Furthermore, *Like A Virgin* was the first album on which Rodgers used the Synclavier, an instrument he would be most enthusiastic about, to the detriment of his guitar playing. Sabino, too, used the Synclavier, but for the most part, stuck to a Sequential Circuits Prophet 5, as well as Fender Rhodes and acoustic piano (the latter most effectively on 'Shoo-Bee-Doo').

When the first single was discussed, Rodgers felt that 'Material Girl' was the obvious choice. But the consensus of opinion (including Madonna's) was that 'Like A Virgin' was the one. I think Rodgers' instincts were right. Either way, both songs were enormous hit singles, as was the album, which remains Madonna's biggest seller.

Rodgers said in *Le Freak* that the album release was delayed owing to Madonna's self-titled debut selling in large quantities on the back of the singles from it. This created an unstoppable head of steam for the album. Four huge hit singles from the album helped maintain growth, as did two non-album singles in 'Crazy For You' and 'Into The Groove'.

As the album was originally sequenced, it does fade in quality after 'Shoo-Bee-Doo'. If you took out the last two tracks on the album and swapped in those two non-album singles, this would have been an even bigger hit record. Of course, 'Into The Groove' was added to the 1985 international reissue, where it opened side two with its effervescent earworm pop.

The irony was not lost on Rodgers that basically the same sound they had been pushing with Chic without recent success was number one, with Madonna fronting it. *Like A Virgin* has some golden songs, including stunning Chic Organisation highlights.

'Material Girl' (Peter Brown/Robert Rans)

This cover was a good fit for Madonna, whose phrasing makes the most of the tongue-in-cheek lyrics. In *Le Freak,* Rodgers handily outlined Madonna's comfortable range as between alto and mezzo-soprano (as on 'Shoo-Bee-Doo' or 'Angel'), so there were challenges on where she opted to go higher, in particular on 'Material Girl'. She sings it in a range from mezzo-soprano up to B-flat, above her comfort zone, and with what Rodgers described as a 'nasal quality'. As an album opener, it does a great job of continuing the sound from *Madonna* while adding the Chic factor that makes it such an irrepressible song.

Thompson's huge, punchy drums open the song, with Edwards sticking close to him for a simple rhythm. Edwards' strong bassline is simple, clear and catchy, which is a fair summary of the verses, too. Edwards only alters his part for the choruses, where his lines are busier, as is the chorus itself. It's a great example of playing for the song.

The melody comes from Rodgers on Synclavier and synth. He gets an almost Bontempi organ sound here that adds a kitsch element. Madonna is simply sensational; her personality shines through and she gives the lyrics her all. She adds her own harmonies to the mix in the chorus for added effect, too. The contrasting backing and harmony vocals of the Simms brothers and Curtis King are equally well done, especially their deadpan chorus singing.

While this is not especially a 'Chic' song, it shows just how well the ensemble can slip into a different style. This thoroughly uplifting and joyous song was the second single from the album and went all the way to number three in Britain and number two in America.

'Angel'

The single did well, reaching number five in Britain and America. It's one of the oldest songs on the album; you can see the links back to her debut quite clearly in its sound and construction. It isn't one of the best tracks, being somewhat repetitive; Madonna has little to work with to give the song extra zip.

It features the alternative core band of Rodgers, Sabino and Bralower. Bralower's drum programming is great for the song, but you have to say that Thompson would have been better and less mechanical. Credit must go to Sabino, who carries all the melody lines and chords on his synth. Rodgers is there, too, doubling him on guitar, but for some reason, he's too low in the mix. When he becomes more audible from 2:26, his guitar adds more life and colour. The outro is the best part of the song, as his guitar finally gets to shine.

'Like A Virgin' (Thomas Kelly/William Steinberg)

Rodgers explained to Howard Massey of *Behind The Glass* in 2000 how he had recorded the title track: 'If you look at the track sheet, you'll see that there aren't very many tracks used. It's just bass, drum kit, one guitar, keyboard pad, one keyboard overdub and Madonna's vocal, plus one other vocal with Madonna to double herself in the chorus only – that's it.'

It's a tricky song vocally for Madonna, singing in the key of F#, which was a stretch for her. But she pulls off a real piece of performance art in that she inhabits the character at the heart of the lyrics. However, with references to 'touched for the very first time' and 'been saving it all for you', it leaves me feeling cold; I think the youthful quality in her vocal is a little discomforting. Musically, I think it lacks a significant uplift in the chorus.

Looking at it from a Chic fan's viewpoint, there's not much about it that reminds me of Chic, in spite of Rodgers, Edwards, Thompson and Sabino playing on it. So all round there's not much for me here. But it was an enormous single, hitting number one in America and many other countries, so it struck a chord with millions of people. It reached number three in Britain, stalling behind the Christmas offerings from Band Aid and Wham!

'Over And Over'

This punchy track is driven by Bralower's exciting, crashing drum programming, which works well alongside great melodic work from Sabino and Rodgers. The latter's chord work is sublime, his guitar chiming through in the mix. Madonna, meanwhile, commands your attention with a confident, assertive vocal.

'Love Don't Live Here Anymore' (Miles Gregory)
This is a brave cover version of the Rose Royce classic. Madonna was up for the challenge, and she recorded it live with the strings and band. She acquits herself well, although her voice isn't as soulful as Gwen 'Rose' Dickey on the original. What she does do well is communicate this story of a relationship ending, left now with 'Just emptiness and memories'. She imbues it with hurt and anguish. Credit also to Rodgers, whose finely detailed string arrangement is immense. Some would have found it hard to follow on from Paul Buckmaster's epic arrangement on the original, but for me, Rodgers surpasses that. Every note is the perfect accompaniment and reaction to Madonna.

'Dress You Up' (Andrea LaRusso/Peggy Stanziale)
Rodgers approached songwriters LaRusso and Stanziale to write a song for Madonna in the Chic style. Why he didn't come up with something himself is a matter of conjecture, but this is a great slice of pop music, nonetheless.

The two verses are strong, with enough details in the lyrics to give Madonna scope for nuances and inflections, such as the delicious 'feel the silky touch of my caresses'. But this is all about the big choruses, which make up the rest of the song and really sell it. Chic fans can enjoy some funky licks from Rodgers, most noticeably in the choruses. He also delivers a piercing rock guitar solo at 2:01. It's unusual for him as he uses the tremolo arm for effect, which he usually shies away from.

'Shoo-Bee-Doo' (Madonna)
Madonna's only solo write on the album is the big one for Chic fans, with a strong but vulnerable vocal performance – she handles it beautifully. It's a gorgeous, reflective song in the verses, especially the wistful opening verse, where she sings purely accompanied by Sabino's piano and what sounds like a string synth. From there, it picks up with a sweet, understated swing to the verses. But when Madonna hits the chorus, it's like the grey clouds have cleared and the sun has come out. It's simply magical as Rodgers' guitar comes in loud and clear and all is right with the world. In the rhythm section, Edwards and Thompson keep it clean and direct, but there's an organic feel to their playing, without the noise of the Synclavier, etc., that lets this song breathe without clutter. There's also a great sax solo from Lenny Pickett for the added icing on the cake. He also plays over the outro. This hidden gem is an outstanding song for Madonna and Chic fans.

'Pretender'
After what seems a long 18-second intro, Madonna comes in with the chorus and it proves to be weak and unmemorable. The verses are better, showcasing a much stronger melody than the chorus as Madonna sings alone, proving more effective. The backing in the verses sees Sabino carrying the melody and Rodgers on rhythm, plus what is otherwise an electronic backing track.

On this occasion, the backing track doesn't particularly work, whereas it does, for example, on 'Over And Over' or 'Dress You Up', where you don't miss the 'real' instruments so much.

The bridge section at 1:19 reminds me of the one in 'Into The Groove' in the way that she slides into it with a more conversational tone, and the melody has a similar feel. It's a really good section, and it's a little disappointing when the chorus comes in after it. Luckily, that bridge section is repeated at 2:27, this time with a post-script about 'his' lying. The outro of more choruses and an instrumental fade of the chorus melody is way too long.

'Stay'

This is not the finish the album needed; it's a B-side at best. There's a positive feel to it, especially in Madonna's and the backing singers' vocals, but the backing track just plods along. It means that the verses, in particular, never quite come to life. So, it leaves the chorus with a lot to do to pick this one up, but this chorus can't manage that. They should have replaced this one on the running order.

B-Movie Matinee (Nile Rodgers) (1985)

Personnel:
Nile Rodgers: lead vocals, guitar, keyboards, backing vocals
Alfa Anderson: lead vocals and backing vocals on 'Let's Go Out Tonight'
Rob Sabino: keyboards
Frank Simms, George Simms, David Spinner, Curtis King: backing vocals
Jimmy Bralower: guitars, bass, drums
Tommy Jymi: keyboards, vocoder
Shizuko Orishige: Japanese Rap on 'Let's Go Out Tonight'
Produced by Nile Rodgers and Tommy Jymi at The Power Station and Atlantic Studios, New York, between May 1984 and early 1985
Release date: June 1985
Label: Warner Bros.
Highest chart places: UK: did not chart, US: did not chart
Running time: 37:20
All songs by Nile Rodgers, except as noted.

Rodgers went from working with Madonna to cutting his second solo album. Meanwhile, Thompson and Edwards had been recording together, but it was clear that there was huge doubt as to whether The Chic Organisation still existed at all as a recording unit. Thompson told *International Musician & Recording World* in October 1985:

> Well, Nile's off doing his thing, and God bless him. I don't know if we'll ever get together again with Nile, but Bernard and I have been talking about doing some things together. Bernard did mention to me that he's thinking about doing another Chic record with Nile, but I don't know. We haven't discussed anything. I think it would be a perfect time for it now. In fact, we have a whole album under wraps that nobody's ever heard. Rhythm tracks, anyway. It's smoking! Bernard and I. Serious stuff, but I don't think anybody will ever get a chance to hear it. It's on the shelf.

The Rogers solo album does feature several Chic alumni, but it's very much a Rodgers solo piece of work. The loosely conceptual theme was the B-movies from the 1950s to the 1970s, packaged in a 3D image of a panic-stricken Rodgers. Original vinyl and CD copies came with 3D glasses to better appreciate the cover.

Musically, at the heart of the album is the Synclavier and Juno 60 played by Rodgers, with Sabino also on Juno 60. Co-producer Tommy 'Rock' Jymi is, in fact, Rodgers' pseudonym, via which he could divert attention from himself to 'Tommy' for the techy esoteric aspects.

The end result is an album which adopts a similar modern computerised approach to *Adventures*. The album does have moments of real magic, the brief return of Alfa Anderson being the absolute highlight. However, the album was not a commercial success. Had it been so, Rodgers had ambitions to tour and the band would have been a mix of the old and the new if he got who he wanted.

'Plan-9' (Rodgers/Bralower)
Rodgers explained the recording process to Gene Santoro: 'Half of all the guitar parts and half of all the bass parts were done by Jimmy Bralower, who sampled guitars and put them into chips in the LinnDrum and made them play all these complex rhythms. Then I did the stereo parts, where I'm playing guitar and bass on the other side. I got that idea from listening to James Brown.'

It's a breezy start to the album, but it's too bright, with the bottom end being too tinny and thin. It's cheerful and listenable enough but lacks anything special to lift it above that. The title is a reference to the cult film *Plan 9 From Outer Space* (1957), directed by Ed Wood.

'State Your Mind' (Martin Celay)
Rodgers told Gene Santoro that Celay was 'an old friend who comes out of the jazz school, like me, so the basic composition was a little tricky to play. The guitar lick was very tricky.' Rodgers masterfully weaves in and around the airy synths over the solid groove. Rodgers also treats us to some jazzy solos that lift the song beautifully. Rodgers' alter ego, Tommy Jymi, is the vocoder voice. The song could have easily graced a 1980s Chic record, and it was released as a single backed with 'Stay Out Of The Light'.

'The Face In The Window' (Eric Lowen/Rick Boston/Dan Navarro)
'That was definitely the most difficult song to record,' Rodgers told Santoro, 'because I wanted it to have my feel, but I also wanted to make the guys who wrote it proud. See, they wrote it as a really rocky kind of thing, power crunch and all. So, I put some power stuff on there, but I also gave it a more subtle kind of approach.' It all makes for a gritty feel on the verses before it breaks into Madonna-style pop for the chorus. That switch isn't as smooth as it could be, so it all comes over like an unfinished demo.

'Doll Squad'
This is all about Edwards' bass, which promises something special until Rodgers comes in with double-tracked rhythm guitars – it all sounds a bit dull and repetitive. The outro is the best part, where Rodgers chants the title over some nice guitar licks. *The Doll Squad* was a 1973 low-budget film directed by Ted V. Mikels.

'Let's Go Out Tonight'
Anderson's guest harmony vocals give this song some welcome extra gloss. The 'Japanese' feel in the melody made Rodgers think of asking Shizuko

Orishige (a recording engineer) to perform the rap parts. It's one of the best songs on the album, showcasing a delightful, sweet chorus and an attractive melody. The part at 3:39, where Rodgers comes in with a high lead part based on the song's melody, giving it an extra push, is clever. Anderson and Rodgers' effervescent, happy vocals make for an upbeat ending, which is finished off with a guitar solo. It was released as a single and got to number 88 in America.

'Groove Master'

Rodgers plays guitar and bass on this one. 'It was the first time I had the confidence to play bass,' he told Santoro, 'but I really like the way it feels.' The title, obviously, promises a lot, but it falls well short of being the ultimate groove track you would hope for. It drives along on an insistent rhythm that fails to really get anything going of note at all. The dullness is broken at 2:03 by guitar effects from Rodgers, who then overlays a solo that piques your interest at last. From there, it's back to more effects, including vocal embellishments. However, none of this is enough to raise the song from the mundane.

'Wavelength'

It's time for a ballad. This stands out from the other songs on the album because of the change of pace, mood and sound. It's a laid-back piece, not unlike Steely Dan in style and composition, and Rodgers' yearning voice underlines that, as do the polished backing vocals. Unfortunately, it's a lacklustre track that succeeds only in changing the album's mood.

'Stay Out Of The Light'

Rodgers revealed to Santoro that he used a 1937 D'Angelico New Yorker guitar on this one: 'I still consider myself a jazz guitarist,' he said, 'because that's what I've studied; that's what I study now.' Amusingly, the song features sampled lines from *Raiders Of The Lost Ark* – 'stop, stay out of the light', 'throw me the whip', 'adios señor' and 'I'll show you what I'm accustomed to, Dr. Jones'. The song itself is a curiously low-key closer to the album. Some of Rodgers' guitar figures hark back to the verses of 'I Want Your Love' or 'Together' – it has a similar, almost sad and wistful feel to it. It's a reasonable enough effort but one you would have expected midway through the sequencing. The last part of the track is extremely effective, courtesy of Rodgers' tasteful overdubbed lead guitar parts.

Chic-Ism (Chic) (1992)

Personnel:
Nile Rodgers: guitar, vocals
Bernard Edwards: bass, vocals
Sylver Logan Sharp: lead vocals (tracks 1, 2, 3, 5, 7, 8, 9, 11, 13)
Jenn Thomas: lead vocals (tracks 1, 3, 6, 7, 8, 10, 11, 13)
Princessa (Jennece S. Moore): lead vocals/rap (tracks 1, 4, 7, 13)
Robin Clark, Michelle Cobbs, Fonzi Thornton, Brenda White King, Tawatha Agee, Briz, Dennis Collins: vocals
Richard Hilton: keyboards, programming
James Preston: keyboards
Andreas Levin: programming
Geraldo Velez: percussion
Sterling Campbell & Sonny Emory: drums
Stan Harrison: alto & tenor saxophone
Steve Elson: alto, tenor & baritone saxophone
Mac Gollehon: trumpet, flugelhorn, piccolo trumpet
Gene Orloff: conductor (strings)
Julien Barber, Elena Barere, Alfred Brown, Max Ellen, Winterton Garvey, Juliet Haffner, Regis Iandiorio, Richard Locker, Matthew Raimondi, Richard Sortomme, Marti Sweet, Mitsue Takayama, Gerald Tarack, Fred Zlotkin: strings
Produced by Nile Rodgers and Bernard Edwards at Power Station, New York, and Skyline Studios, New York, in 1991
Release date: 3 March 1992
Label: Warner Bros.
Highest chart places: UK: did not chart, US: did not chart
Running time: 62:47
All songs by Edwards and Rodgers, except as noted.

The return of Chic was heralded in a half-hearted way with the over-fussy 'Jack Le Freak' (a concoction of 'Le Freak') in 1987, which made the UK top 20. Plans were put in motion for a reunion after a jam on 'Good Times' and 'Le Freak' at Rodgers' 36th birthday party at the China Club in New York. According to Fonzi Thornton, in *Easlea*, Rodgers, Edwards, Thornton, Martin and Anderson played together. On keyboards was Paul Shaffer, along with his fellow member of the Letterman Show House Band, Anton Fig, on drums.

Rodgers and Edwards duly went ahead with the Chic 'reunion', principally the two of them plus the return of Fonzi Thornton, Gene Orloff, Geraldo Velez and a familiar coterie of backing singers. They apparently tried to bring Ray Jones back on keyboards, but none of the other key players were invited.

Choosing the new vocalists was a long, hard slog. Eventually, they picked the imposing Sylver Logan Sharp, whose alto voice made for a different in tone and feel from Anderson or Martin. Twenty-five more singers were tried out to partner with Sharp. In the end, they took her suggestion to try out her friend Jenn Thomas, whom she had sung with before in a band called Brown's Creation. Thomas was the perfect choice to work alongside Sharp, the two having contrasting voices that blended well and offered a change of style when they sang separate leads.

There was a big media push on this album to restore Chic as a top-drawer act, including a TV appearance in 1992 on the UK's prime-time *Jonathan Ross* chat show. Ross, clearly a fan, was keen to know why the band had disintegrated the first time around. A diplomatic Edwards explained: 'We were making so many records and got kinda tired and burned out and we wanted to go out individually and see what we could do.' Ross's next question – why now? – elicited this response: 'It felt like the right time', Edwards explained. 'We had been apart seven years, and we got together at his (Rodgers's) birthday party. It felt really great, so we thought, let's try it again.' The band ran through two songs – these being 'Chic Mystique' and 'Good Times', which closed the show. It seemed that 'happy days are here again' as 'Good Times' has it!

However, the album fell short with its 'un-Chic-like' sound. Part of the issue was the 'updated' production style, which sounds harsher than the more organic sound of the past. The songs themselves have their moments, and there are one or two stand-outs; it's interesting that the better-crafted tracks are the ballads. You can see from the credits that there was a considerable effort to make this something like a Chic album. The strings make a return with Gene Orloff conducting, the brass section is back and then there's the familiar list of backing singers. One or more of these singing the lead would have stamped the album's identity, but instead, Rodgers and Edwards opted for the r&b voices of Sharp and Thomas. The raps are understandable inclusions for the time but are nothing remarkable.

Stan Harrison, who played alto and tenor saxophone on the album, sadly regrets that 'I have no memory of the Chic session. Steve Elson (saxophone), Mac Gollehan (trumpet) and I would have been together at the session. Recording as a unit was usually the case unless you were booked just for soloing. We are the only horn players on the record. I must say this: Nile is a great producer and wonderful to work for/with. He is always open to suggestions, always makes people comfortable and he always gets the most from the musicians he hires because of this.'

Due to it coming out primarily on CD, the extra running time allowed for more filler to be included. But even if trimmed, it would have struggled to recapture past glories because little here reaches that gold standard. It is a considerable update of the old Chic sound but lacks the charm. TV appearances and press helped push initial interest, but praise was superficial, focusing on how great it was to have Chic back without saying the album wasn't so hot. The public weren't sold on 'Chic Mystique' either – the single only climbed to number 48 in the UK. The knock-on effect was that the album didn't chart in the UK or on the *Billboard* chart in America.

'Chic Mystique' (Rodgers/Edwards/Princessa)
The song samples Kurtis Blow's 1984 hit, 'AJ Scratch'. It was the single, a calling card for the album, released in a large number of formats and combinations. Edwards is pure dynamite from the opening notes. That's the good news. The bad news is that the 'hit it' sample wears thin, as do the pounding drums. It is, however, a great introduction to Sharp and Thomas, who trade lines and harmonise well together. I like the melody and chord sequences, but it feels too stodgy in the rhythm section and the chorus seems weaker than the verses. There is a kind of breakdown at 4:21, which centres on Edwards' bass, but it's too short, although the strings are at their best from here on. Right at the end of the outro (at 6:26), the 'ah' from 'Le Freak' is featured – a nice reference to former glories.

There was a bonus track version of Sharp's acappella vocals included on some of the single releases. It's not essential listening, but it is a nice showcase of Sharp's passionate vocals.

'Your Love'
We are then treated to a lightning-fast segue into this instantly better song, with Rodgers' scratchy rhythm harking back to his familiar best work. Sharp turns in a great r&b style vocal, which blends well with the sweet-toned backing vocals. The harmonies over the lead vocal are superb. There's a brief sax solo and some welcome Chic strings work to follow it. They enhance the track, taking off and flying in what is an echo of the parts on 'I Want Your Love'. It's an above-average track that needed a stronger hook in the chorus to improve it.

'Jusagroove'
Sharp and Thomas share the lead vocals over an instrumental backdrop that reflects the title in its groove. Edwards shines with supple, elastic bass playing as Rodgers' riff drives things along. The pair are a party on their own! While technically, this is a tour de force, and the ladies throw themselves into the vocals, it falls short of being a great song.

'Something You Can Feel' (Rodgers/Edwards/Princessa)
It was, with hindsight, inevitable that Rodgers and Edwards would explore rap, and Princessa's lyrics are a homage to the Chic 'effect'. It starts promisingly enough with a James Brown-style funk rhythm featuring Velez's percussion and Rodgers' scratchy guitar. Then in comes Princessa, who no doubt delivers her lyrics well, but her rap style is not for me. It sounds like she is clashing with the Chic backing track. The strings add the top note accents and there's lovely flute work, but as a song, I feel this is a style and form that doesn't fit them well.

'One And Only One'
A very welcome change of pace for the first ballad, Rodgers plays exquisite jazzy guitar and Sharp's sensitive, heartfelt vocal is supported by high

harmony vocals from the Chic choir. This is, in effect, 'A Warm Summer Night' for the 1990s and is easily one of the best songs on the album. Anderson and Martin would have loved this song.

'Doin' That Thing To Me'

The instrumentation is mostly sublime, apart from the over-loud solid thwack of the drums. But the vocal line is less memorable. It's Thomas who takes the lead vocal, but she is stuck with a lifeless arrangement.

'Chicism' (Rodgers/Edwards/Princessa)

Another example of Chic self-mythology. Did we need another? On this track and 'In It To Win It', Rodgers makes use of his wah-wah pedal. He told *Guitar Player* in June 1992 his 'secret': 'Never keep time with the pedal. Use it for expression and keep time with your hands. The greatest example of that kind of playing is 'Theme From Shaft'. You leave it down for a certain amount of time and use it for emphasis. Every now and then, I'll keep time with it to do a train effect, but most of the time, I make it wah only when I want it to wah.'

The opening audience applause and vocal introduction call to mind 'Chic Cheer'. The band tear out of the traps with fizzing energy, and it would have been an obvious opening track, but they perhaps felt they had to open with the big radio-featured single instead. Princessa raps again, but it works here as she is part of the overall sound rather than the band backing her. Most of the musical interest comes from Rodgers' effervescent rhythm playing; the sledgehammer drum beat crushes much else in the way of finesse, leaving the track without any small details or subtleties.

'In It To Win It'

By now, it's obvious that Rodgers and Edwards are at the top of their game as musicians. This is yet more excellent work from the pair, but, as is often the case on this album, the drums dominate the centre of the sound. Thomas takes the bulk of the lead vocals. Sharp joins in for the chorus on lead (she opens the song alone with the chorus) and the combined effect of the two together is effective as their voices blend together beautifully. The last minute or so of the song (from 4:05), with the two trading lines, is superb. It's a good song, but it would benefit immensely from a remix softening the drums.

'My Love's For Real'

The familiar chattering guitar of Rodgers opens this song with the chorus sung by the choir. A lick from Edwards leads into a little instrumental section that is prime Chic, with the brass and strings on fine form. The dive down from the strings into the first verse is a killer touch. Sharp gets to take the verses and her phrasing is top quality. So, we have a familiar Chic contrast of solo-sung verses and choir-sung choruses – a technique that has served the band well. The strings and the backing choir help seal this as one which is right up there with their earlier work.

'Take My Love'

An absolutely terrific lead vocal from Thomas on this torch song could perhaps render the backing immaterial, such is the compelling nature of her performance. The chorus is spine-tingling as the backing vocals come in for a well-thought-out, beautiful arrangement. The strings are lushly fabulous and the drums/percussion give the right amount of dynamics. Rodgers, for his part, delivers those sweet little jazz licks for extra texture. They save the best for last with a breakdown from 4:34 to the end. It's down to just Thomas, the backing vocals, Velez's percussion, piano and synth. Stripped down like this, Thomas's voice shines even more. A long, cool fade to silence almost provokes a little clap – an outstanding track.

'High'

One of the better tracks on the album, this has an almost weightless feel and even the drums are slightly less forceful. Sharp and Thomas duet on vaporous lead vocals, but you can also clearly hear Thornton's and Edwards' harmonies in the choruses. The best part comes at 2:35 when a funkier groove comes in via wicked clavinet from Hilton or Preston. Rodgers' precision riffing is equally worthy, but in the final analysis, this is a song that, with a more sympathetic drums/percussion part, would have been much better.

'M.M.F.T.C.F.'

The lyrics reveal the acronym of the title, 'Make my funk the Chic funk'. Rodgers told Chris Gill of *Guitar Player* in 1992: 'On 'M.M.F.T.C.F.', I was trying to bring back a lost art. When I started playing guitar, there were hit records like 'Scorpio', where guitars played the melody with chords. They were sexy. I don't hear that at all on records nowadays.' 'Scorpio' by Dennis Coffey & The Detroit Guitar Band (which reached the dizzy heights of number six on the US singles chart) is required listening for anyone interested in the development of Rodgers' playing.

This is a jaunty instrumental, with the only vocal being the ensemble vocalists reciting the title in full. The drums, as ever, are a pain, but apart from that, this is a good track. Rodgers's lead and rhythm playing stand out. The strings sound every bit as great as they usually do on Chic records.

'Chic Mystique (Reprise)' (Rodgers/Edwards/Princessa)

A pointless reprise. You can see the idea of it top and tailing the album, but this adds nothing at all, being little more than an edit of the opening track.

Chic Freak And More Treats (Nile Rodgers) (1996)

Personnel:
Nile Rodgers: guitar, backing vocals
Bernard Edwards: bass
Richard Hilton & Chazz Oliver: keyboards, programming
Omar Hakim: drums
Sylver Logan Sharp: lead vocals (tracks 1, 2, 4, 8-10, 13)
Christopher Max: lead vocals (tracks 3, 10, 13)
Ashford & Simpson: lead vocals ('Upside Down')
Simon Le Bon & The Crowell Sisters: lead vocals ('Do That Dance')
Taja Sevelle: lead vocals ('He's The Greatest Dancer')
Wayne Thompson: rap ('Do That Dance (Dancehall Rap)')
Christine Gordon, Suzette Henry, Jill Jones, Audra Lomax Parker, Tanya Ramtulla: backing vocals
Produced by Nile Rodgers and Chazz Oliver at Le Crib Studios, Westport, Sony Studios, New York, Right Track Recording, New York, in 1996
Release date: 1996 (re-released in 2003 by A 440 Music Group)
Label: Video Arts Music
Highest chart places: UK: did not chart, US: did not chart
Running time: 61:00
All songs written by Edwards and Rodgers, except as noted.

This was mostly (all but one song) recorded prior to the Budokan gigs in April 1996. These are detailed in the following *Live At The Budokan* entry. The album was originally released in Japan only, following on from those concerts. It was never intended for worldwide release, but the inevitable happened!

Although the release was likely intended in advance (rather than a cash-in), you could question whether it was a suitable tribute to Edwards. If it was, he deserved better than this difficult album to love, with needlessly updated versions of Chic classics and songs they did for other artists. Credit to them for trying some different approaches, but generally, they lack the style, charm and conviction of the originals. The only positives on the album are that Sylver Logan Sharp is, as ever, a great singer and one of the new songs, 'Just One World', is pretty good. Musically, the core band are fine, but the guest vocalists add nothing special to the songs. The three lesser-known singers are Christopher Max, the Crowell Sisters and Taja Sevelle. Max had signed a deal with EMI, which saw his debut album, *More Than Physical* (1989), produced and played on by Rodgers. The Crowell Sisters' only album, *Crowell Sisters* (complete with a cover of 'We Are Family'), came out in 1996 in Japan. Rodgers also produced and played on it. His connection to Sevelle was that he co-wrote a song with her for her 1997 *Toys Of Vanity* album.

The front cover of the original version was a small shot of Rodgers on a red background. The international edition, however, was a ridiculously large blow-up of a list of the celebrity names involved.

'Everybody Dance'
A horrible intro and a synthetic sound can't quite completely dull the song. Oddly, Rodgers mixes himself so low as to be inaudible. Edwards fares better; his bass is still up in the mix. He gets his solo, too, though it's quite different to the original, with wah-wah backing from Rodgers (audible at last). Sharp is the big plus on this – she gives it her all but still can't save the song.

'Dance Dance Dance' (Edwards/Kenny Lehman/Rodgers)
Rodgers' guitar is the main intro and all sounds potentially good until the thumping drum track comes in. Edwards, meanwhile, seems free to roam and play whatever he feels. His licks and runs are a pleasure, but this is still a leaden mess of a song. Sharp deserves credit for another strong performance.

'Let's Dance' (Bowie)
Christopher Max tries hard, but he just isn't up to this at all. This is a truly awful remake, with a fog-thick, dense bottom end. Anything you like about the song, such as the catchy melody, the brass and Bowie's well-judged vocal, is systematically ruined here. For example, the 'if you say run, I'll run with you' section, which was a high point of the original, is utterly dreadful. It loses the sublime melody of the original.

'Le Freak'
Sylver is back on vocals and this is one where there are some interesting variations. The strings are programmed, as are the brass parts, but there is a nice harmony brass part which drifts in and out against the main melody in the choruses. What it lacks is the groove and dynamics of the original. This is very noticeable during the dense, thick instrumental break.

'Upside Down'
Singers Nickolas Ashford and Valerie Simpson, successful contemporaries of Rodgers and Edwards from the 1970s, are interesting choices, but they never really 'own' the song. The 'hopping' rhythm on the original is over-accentuated and messy here. It's a painful listen, with the vocals trying to imitate the original tune, which battles to be heard in the busy, harsh-sounding mix.

'Do That Dance' (Le Bon/Garrett Oliver/Tanya Ramtulla/Rodgers)
This new song has a bit of old-time Chic style in the intro! Sadly, it doesn't last and the song is dragged down by the soupy bottom end. The Crowell Sisters' curiously lifeless vocals don't add the requisite joy, either. There's a quick motif from 'I Want Your Love' at 2:08 before Simon Le Bon comes in, sounding utterly out of his depth, although it is a step up in vitality. This is an extremely limited song that took four people to write! It was featured in the Budokan show.

'He's The Greatest Dancer'
Taja Sevelle takes the microphone. The musicality and charm of the original are missing, and when it comes to Sevelle's solo lead vocal, she just doesn't communicate it with any conviction.

'Good Times'
Sharp is back again, so at least the vocal is credibly good. The mix is off, with Sharp too low, and the clarity and punch of the original song are lacking. Edwards throws in some trademark licks, which are the musical highlights. Sadly, the breakdown (3:11) is a real wreck, with dull guitar and no emphasis at all on Edwards, which is the final insult.

'I Want Your Love'
While this isn't a patch on the original, Sharp does sing it really well and the backing track is somewhere in the vicinity of the original. What we get is a kind of lighter copy, but this still ends up being the best of a bad bunch.

'Music Is My House' (Oliver/Rodgers)
Christopher Max is back again, this time singing with Sharp on what is an energetic but tediously dull song.

'We Are Family'
Sharp is up again on this slowed-down travesty. The sound is ponderous, as though the brakes are on. Nothing works well on it and even Sharp can't rescue it. Her vocals sound just plain wrong at this slower tempo.

'Do That Dance (Dancehall Rap)' (Le Bon/Garrett Oliver/Tanya Ramtulla/Rodgers)
A reworking of the earlier song to an even less positive effect, with Wayne Thompson contributing a rap (in place of Simon Le Bon). This must be the absolute nadir of Nile Rodgers' career.

'Just One World' (Gordon/Oliver/Rodgers)
Of the three new songs, this is easily the best and Sharp, for one, knows it. Sharp sings it with Christopher Max, and, in fact, this *is* the Budokan 1996 performance edited and disguised by cutting off the intro and outro! The full version (on *YouTube*) is even better, but not sonically as great. This edit has a rich mix to it that showcases the vocals and music perfectly. It's a ballad of sorts with a good feel, and the vocal pair are excellent together.

Related Song
'Let's Bounce' (Rodgers/Nataraj/Erick Sermon)
This was featured in the 2001 film *Rush Hour 2* during the end credits but didn't make the soundtrack album. It was recorded after the *Chic Freak*

album, but it sounds like the same band playing, although it will be Jerry Barnes on bass. The lead vocalist is Erick Sermon, but you can clearly hear Sylver Logan Sharp on harmonies.

It's nothing special, relying strongly on a lacklustre chorus, which strangely lacks any 'bounce'. The rap is underwhelming; I'd rather hear just Sharp. Rodgers is pretty invisible and it all sounds like a cash-grab recording. Co-writer Nataraj is the alias for one Herbie Tribino. He also played around the same time with the We Are Family Collective, which raised funds for the 9/11 victims, survivors and families.

Live At The Budokan (Chic) (1999)

Personnel:
Nile Rodgers: guitar, vocals
Bernard Edwards: bass, vocals
Richard Hilton: keyboards
Omar Hakim: drums
Gerardo Velez: percussion
Bill Holloman: saxophone
Mac Gollehon: trumpet
Philippe Saisse: piano
Sylver Logan Sharp: lead vocals
Jill Jones & Christopher Max: backing vocals
Debbie, Joni & Kim Sledge: lead vocals (on the Sister Sledge medley)
Steve Winwood: lead vocals, organ (on 'Stone Free')
Slash: lead guitar (on 'Le Freak' and 'Stone Free')
Recorded at The Budokan Theatre, Tokyo, 18 April 1996
Release date: 23 February 1999
Label: Sumthing Else
Highest chart places: UK: did not chart, US: did not chart
Running time: 66:53
Setlist: 'Le Freak', 'Dance, Dance, Dance', 'I Want Your Love', 'He's The Greatest Dancer', 'We Are Family', 'Do That Dance', 'Good Times/Rapper's Delight', 'Stone Free', 'Chic Cheer'. Also played were 'Let's Dance' and 'Just One World' – places in the running order uncertain.

In *Le Freak,* Rodgers states that Chic were 'newly reformed' for the concerts. He also makes it clear that this was to be a new start for Chic and not a one-off. The band were put together for a three-day series of shows in April 1996, tying in with Rodgers' award as JT's (Japan Tobacco's) Super Producer of the Year. Rodgers invited Edwards along and assembled a band drawn from the *Chic-Ism* sessions, along with new recruits such as Jill Jones, who sang lead with Sylver Logan Sharp.

Joining the band was saxophonist Bill Holloman: 'I usually play a Selma Mark VI saxophone, although, in the Budokan show, I am playing an LA Sax because I had an endorsement with them. I played a Yamaha sax for a while when my Selma got beat up on one of the trips.' Holloman adds: 'That was the first tour I did with Nile. We rehearsed for about three weeks and they were really cool.' He recalls that it was Edwards who ran the rehearsals: 'Bernard was the band leader. He was the one stopping and starting the tunes and all that kind of stuff.'

Holloman says that the setlist 'wasn't difficult to put together because we played the hits. This was before we started adding some other stuff. We had guests. Simon (Le Bon) sang 'Let's Dance' because he had worked with Nile in Duran Duran and, of course, the song was one Nile had worked on with

Bowie.' That song wasn't used for the CD or DVD release, and it seems a stretch to have even used Le Bon. Also missing from the recordings was a lovely version of 'Just One World', which you can find on YouTube and as audio on *Chic Freak & More Treats.*

The most baffling guest stars are Slash and Steve Winwood, and covering Jimi Hendrix was even more strange. At least there was the Kathy-less Sister Sledge, who added the right sort of extra sparkle to proceedings. The final performance was a two-hour-long televised special which, tragically, was overshadowed by the death of Bernard Edwards.

Prior to the final show, Edwards was sick with what he referred to onstage later as the 'Hong Kong Flu'. Medical advice was that he should not play the show. While Rodgers accepted that as the correct course of action, Edwards was having none of it. Instead, he got a vitamin shot and promised to go to the hospital after the show. He made it through the first half until 'Let's Dance' before passing out, and yet somehow he came back onstage to continue. For the second half, he played sitting down, only stepping out for the choreographed sections. Rodgers was aware that his partner was struggling and digging deep to make it through without letting the performance drop.

With the show over, Edwards didn't go to the hospital but instead retired to his bed to sleep off his illness. Rodgers recalled in *Le Freak* that he (Rogers) had been thrown out of bed at 1:33 am by what he thought was an earthquake. Later, he felt that the jolt was Edwards' passing, the time of death confirmed by the medical examiner as being within the period of 1 to 2 am. The cause of death was cited as pneumonia. Nobody else in the touring party was informed of Edwards' death at the time. Holloman confirms: 'We didn't find out until we got home. I was back in South Carolina when I got a call from our sound engineer. We all knew he was sick that night, but he seemed a little better after the show.'

The recorded performance is, therefore, a hard watch. Given it is a celebration of Chic's music, the setlist is understandably mostly greatest hits, save for the puzzling 'Stone Free'. Sister Sledge acquit themselves well as guest vocalists on their medley section, while the less said about Slash's guitar work on 'Le Freak', the better!

It was the end of an era. Sammy Figueroa feels that 'there was an alchemical vibe when those two guys were in the studio producing. When Bernard died, a lot of things were not the same. Nile told me he thought that would be the end of him in the business. Nile finally got his own identity, but his foundation is always the grooves he had created with Bernard.'

Nile Rodgers & Chic – The New Era

Rodgers' initial steps with a new band were back in Japan in 1997, a year after Edwards' passing. Holloman recalls:

> I bumped into Joe Worthing, who had been the production manager on that (Budokan) show. He said, 'I think we're going back', and then Nile called me. I was sceptical because I didn't know how you could replace Bernard Edwards, but if anyone came close, it was Jerry (Barnes). Jerry, I think, was the key to Nile coming back; if he hadn't found somebody that great, I don't think Nile would have done it. Once we started to rehearse, I thought it was going to work. The Blue Note clubs wanted us to come over and play, and this time around, we were doing longer shows, so we added one or two things. We went to Japan for a month and we played every Blue Note gig, and at that time, there were five of them. It was a rugged trip because we played two shows a night.

There were more gigs following Japan, running up to what was intended to be the final ever Chic show at Tramps in New York on 3 April 1998. Yet, Rodgers had a change of heart, and perhaps the words of his late partner at that Budokan concert were part of that. He recalled to Imogen O'Rourke for *The Guardian* on 13 December 1999: 'Bernard was looking at the audience and he turns to me and says, 'You know, this thing is bigger than us', and I had no idea what he was talking about, but I see it now.' So began a new era for the band, which continues to this day.

Holloman saw Rodgers' development: 'It took Nile a little while to really be great in that (band leader) role, which he certainly is now. Not in terms of music but in terms of entertainer and frontman. All the stuff that he does now.'

The touring band stabilised for some years around the twin lead vocals of Sylver Logan Sharp and Jessica (Jessie) Wagner. Wagner recalls:

> I joined in 2003. I met Omar (Hakim) through a family friend. I was moving to New York and he liked what I was writing. And he said, 'You know, Chic are looking for a singer; let me introduce you.' So he took me to Nile's office and he asked me if I would be interested in doing an audition. We did 'I'm Coming Out' and it seemed like I harmonised. The next thing I know, I am on a Japanese tour and that was my trial by fire. It was my first tour ever and Chic were big in Japan. I got lucky because they were already deciding to go with this other girl when Omar said, 'Let's try out Jessie.' They liked the look and sound of me, Sylver and Cherie (Mitchell on keyboards/vocals), so that's why they went with me.

The band then featured (and still do) a two-piece horn section but no string section. Wagner explains how the strings were (and are) covered:

> Rich (Hilton) played a lot of the string lines. He's like Nile's right-hand man in a lot of ways for the music. When they put the songs and the arrangement together, Rich was always in the mix. He did a lot of the groundwork. Chic music is huge and lush; he really wanted to have that beautiful, rich sound. Between Cherie (Mitchell) and Rich, it gave us the complete fullness that we needed.

Bill Holloman explains the arrangements: 'Nile was his own arranger, of course. Rich came up with parts, so did Jerry and so did I. There are still some little spots in the live show that were my ideas. Nile was very open to good ideas.'

The brass parts required considerable work to arrange because, as Holloman explains ...

> ... there isn't that much horn stuff in the original Chic music. I didn't get a lot of guidance, so, anyway, basically, what I did was sketch out the string parts because I felt the way Nile and Bernard used the strings was pretty much the way they used horns. A lot of the stabs the strings were doing would have been horns in the 1960s. So, I started playing my parts and people seemed to dig it. We were kind of a three-man section, really; there were the two horn players and Rich (Hilton). We played a lot of the same stuff together. That's what Richard mostly did. We were locked into what we were doing; otherwise, it would have been a cacophony. So, on 'I Want Your Love', we played the whole line, the strings, and not just the brass part on the record.

Holloman saw other opportunities, too: 'When we rehearsed 'I'm Coming Out', there's a trombone solo on the record, but I just took it because we didn't have a trombone. It became a sax solo.'

Wagner learned a lot from Sharp about how to present herself on stage: 'She would take pictures and she would call me into the room and say, 'Jessie, look at this, I want you to see what you're doing there.' She really talked me through what it was like to share a stage with somebody and handle the mic properly. She helped me to handle the stage in a more professional way.' Wagner enjoyed her solo spots: 'I loved being able to come out. Sylver is a fantastic vocalist and we did blend really well, but there's nothing like it when you get a moment for yourself. The crowd would always be floored by the time we got to 'We Are Family' – it was such a huge ending to the medley. Then, for 'He's The Greatest Dancer', I got to dance with Geraldo (Velez) and that was a highlight because he had more energy than the rest of us.' One secret ace the band had vocally was Cherie Mitchell, who added vocal support and played keyboards. Wagner recalls Mitchell as 'a great singer and a fun, vibrant person. Probably the most laid-back woman I have ever met. She looks cool and she is cool. I don't remember Cherie getting upset about anything.'

There was one spectacular time when things went wrong, says Wagner:

> We lost the key we were in and I, of course, couldn't control my face. We got through it and Sylver said, after we finished the song, '…or something like that', and I just died laughing. With some artists, if that happened, you would never hear the end of it, but Nile was laughing. That was the beauty of Nile; he would let things blow off and he didn't take anything too seriously. He knew everyone was on stage to do the best that they possibly could.

The lineup with Sharp and Wagner had four live albums/DVDs released. The band consisted of Nile Rodgers (guitar, vocals), Jerry Barnes (bass, vocals), Richard Hilton (keyboards), Sylver Logan Sharp (lead vocals), Jessica Wagner (lead vocals), Cherie Mitchell (keyboards, vocals), Omar Hakim (drums), Gerardo Velez (percussion), Bill Holloman (saxophone) and Mac Gollehon (trumpet). The Amsterdam show saw a couple of changes to the lineup, as we will see.

The first release saw the band's entire set, as part of the *Best Disco In Town* UK tour of 2003, featured on a DVD compilation of the same name from Icestorm Entertainment. It showcased all the artists on the tour at the Wembley Arena show in London. 'That was pretty exciting', says Wagner. 'We got to wear these really cool Sun Treacy hats. That was just an electric show.' The set, as still is the norm, kicks off with an intro and then a long pause, the band standing stock still facing the back of the stage before launching into 'Everybody Dance'. Wagner laughs at the memory: 'The longer we stayed there, the bigger the frenzy would get!'

The latter three live albums were originally released on the Sumthing Else label, which was a company originally set up by Rodgers for his work on video game music. The first of these was *Mount Fuji,* recorded at the Mount Fuji Festival, Oyama, Japan, on 24 August 2003. This was released on CD and DVD and covers the usual set of the era with no extra surprises. Next came *Live At Montreux,* recorded at the Jazz Festival on 17 July 2004, also on CD and DVD. The main bonus here is the inclusion of 'At Last I Am Free'. Finally, there's *A Night In Amsterdam,* recorded at the Paradiso on 17 July 2005. This notably includes 'Thinking Of You' ('one of my favourites', says Wagner) and 'At Last I Am Free'. Holloman took a fabulous front-of-stage solo for 'At Last I Am Free'. 'That was fun', he says. 'It came out of rehearsals. Nothing was happening at that point in the song, so I just started playing, and that became my solo. Unfortunately, we didn't keep it in the set for very long. It stayed until Sylver and Jessie left. When the new girls came in, it wasn't revived, which was too bad because I always enjoyed doing it, and it was a nice change of pace in the show.' Wagner recalls two other set changes in her era: 'The last change I remember was 'My Feet Keep Dancing' – we did it once or twice. One time, we did 'Spacer', too.' The latter featured a tasty sax solo before the riff intro while Nile would 'purport' (says Holloman) to tune his guitar.

A welcome extra presence at Amsterdam was Fonzi Thornton, who, says Wagner, 'would come back for certain shows, especially whenever we did television productions like the first VH-1 Honours awards. He was always at anything we did for the We Are Family Foundation.' Barry Johnson is the other change at Amsterdam, covering on bass for the indisposed Jerry Barnes. Holloman notes: 'They tried a few different bass players while Jerry was gone for a while. I don't know why he was away; I just know that we missed him. Barry is an excellent bass player, but Jerry had put his stamp on the sound.' Wagner says 'Jerry had some things he needed to take care of and then he came back. Barry was like Jerry in that he would always have me laughing on stage.' We can see such a moment in Amsterdam during the intro of 'At Last I Am Free', where Johnson plays a wrong note to amuse Wagner. Wagner says the brass section were always fun, too: 'Whenever I would go over to that side of the stage, I would look at Bill. We would always talk about his hair – he has the best hair ever. Curt (Ramm, who replaced Mac Gollehon) was kind of like a jokester, too. But they played the part of the cool jazz cats.' *Amsterdam* is a strong performance, probably the best of the live albums. The Sumthing Else sets have turned up on other labels since then under various titles, usually along the lines of *Best Of Chic live.*

All of the shows are a great record of the band live, and they are remarkably consistent. When asked for highlights of her time with the band, Wagner said: 'It's hard to distinguish individual concerts; I really enjoyed playing in Ghent because we played on a bridge and there were people floating under us. It was one of the most beautiful sights I had ever seen.'

Since then, the band have substantially changed, with only Rodgers, Barnes and Hilton left from the era that produced those live recordings. Holloman was ...

> ... surprised that Omar (Hakim) stayed as long as he did because he's so great. That's not to belittle anything or anybody, but he's had such a big career. He was with the band for about ten years. In the early years, after 1997, we didn't work a whole lot. There were some years when we maybe played ten gigs. It was nothing like what they do now or at the end of my time in the band. I finally thought I was too old for the amount of touring, even though I'm technically not as old as Nile. He still loves it, but I just got burned out being on the road. I still love Nile, the music and everything.

Why did Wagner leave? 'To be honest, I think I was a little jealous', she says:

> I wanted more time and I just wanted to grow a little bit more. When the Kid Rock opportunity came along, it was a really difficult decision to make because Chic had given me my start. Nile had taken a chance on me; I was

> completely green. So, for a minute, I was gonna try and juggle it, but there was no way I could do that because there were too many conflicts with scheduling.

Sharp has recorded solo, most notably the dancefloor filler 'All This Time' (2004) with Jonathan Peters, which is a testament to her vocal power and a great song. As well as singing with Kid Rock, Wagner has put out albums in her own right, including the rootsy, diverse *Shoes Droppin'* (2020), which features Bill Holloman. She has also been performing a Donna Summer tribute show! Wagner opines that Chic still 'put on a phenomenal show' and that she 'filled in for Folami when she wasn't available, so they know they can call on me if they need backup. I am 100% happy to jump in whenever they need me.'

Since Folami's time as lead vocalist, Kimberly Davis has been the lead, along with Audrey Martells, for some years now. Davis was alerted to the auditions for a new vocalist by her friend, Chic drummer Ralph Rolle. Davis's account to James Potter of *Totally Wired* in July 2021 of the state of the band at the time of her audition and the reaction to her was very revealing:

> The guys in the band would tell me all the time, 'You raised the bar for what we're doing.' Initially, Nile wanted to stop doing Chic. He was so depressed and sick about the band that he just wanted to stop doing it. They all just weren't happy, so they said to Nile, 'You don't give up playing, you just switch up the band.' And so that's what he did. He switched up the band and now we're family for real. We laugh together, we cry together, we live with each other more than our own families. So you know, we are family.

Davis also shared: 'I'm just helping him (Rodgers) live his best life. When I sing 'Get Lucky', he gives me this intro about how he almost died from cancer, and now he feels like the luckiest man alive. So, I'm just helping him to relay his story and that's all I need.'

I'll Be There & Back In The Old School (Chic featuring Nile Rodgers) (Warner Bros., 2015)

Nile Rodgers and Chic were (and are) a big draw live, but did they feel that the need, or desire, to record a new studio album was hanging over them? Holloman says: 'I guess I didn't know whether that would have any legs if he did one. I considered it more of a live act. I think it was different for the singers and stuff.' On 16 February 2001, Rodgers informed the audience at B. B. King's Blues Club in New York that a new album would be released later that year. Wagner says: 'The whole time I was there, there was always talk of putting an album out. One time, we were in Stockholm, and we recorded some vocals. I thought there was going to be a Chic album, but that didn't happen. But what he did later with Kim (Davis) and Folami was amazing.'

Those vocal sessions were at Polar Studios in July 2003, which means backing tracks must have been laid down there or earlier. Rumours eventually settled on a final release date in 2006, but this also came and went.

Rodgers next announced in 2013 that he was working on a new Chic album, which would utilise material left over from the early years. This was firmed up with the arrival of a new single on 20 March 2015. 'I'll Be There' and 'Back In The Old School' were recorded in 2014 and had plenty of vintage Chic about them, with the return of some old friends. Alas, the songs proved to be a false dawn when the album emerged.

'I'll Be There' (Edwards/Rodgers)

This song reminds you of why you loved Chic in the first place. Rodgers unveiled the song during the vernal equinox and total solar eclipse on 20 March 2015 to signify the new beginning for Chic as a recording outfit. Although it makes heavy use of samples from old Chic Organisation tunes, most notably 'Got To Love Somebody', there was real old-style magic in the song. This was helped in no small part by Alfa Anderson, Luci Martin and Fonzi Thornton, who returned to share lead and backing vocals with the then-current Chic vocalists Folami Ankoanda-Thompson and Kimberly Davis. Norma Jean Wright and Robin Clark also appeared in the old recordings. Davis, speaking to *Wax Poetics* in 2015, was thrilled to be singing with Anderson and Martin: 'That was historical, having the originators and us in the same room singing.' Martin responded, 'It's a good thing; I don't want to live in the past, but it's a nice place to visit.' Alfa Anderson gave a fuller summary of the reunion to Christian Wikane for *Pop Matters* in December 2018:

> It took everything that I had not to cry because it was such a powerful moment. I couldn't believe I was back where it all began. I spent a good bit of time in Studio B working on those Chic songs that became such huge hits. I thought about those who are no longer with us, like Bernard, Tony (Thompson) and Raymond (Jones). When I saw Nile, we shared a big hug. At one point, I didn't know if I was going to be able to sing because I was getting so choked up. I had to work through it quietly. It was a wonderful experience to be there. The respect from Nile, Kim and Folami was very evident. The camaraderie that I had with Fonzi and with Luci – I felt like I was home.

Holloman loves the song: 'I remember that one best. I played all the horns on it.' Sadly, no other musician credits have been released for the song, but Bernard Edwards does seem to be featured.

It is a fabulous song, right from the intro – the rumbling bass, percussion, Rodgers' guitar and the intoned 'into the disco scene'. The command and delivery of the vocal lines is vintage Chic, sounding as fresh as ever. An added bonus is the brass led by Holloman, and all that's missing to make it perfect is an authentic string section. I found it hard to listen to the song at first because I didn't want to be let down. But it delivered way more than I thought it would. It's superb, delivering infectious joy in every note and vocal.

There is an instrumental take, plus an extended version, which runs over a minute longer.

'Back In The Old School' (Rodgers/Thomas Troelsen)

The second of the new songs, paving the way for *It's About Time,* is nowhere near as top drawer as 'I'll Be There'. That being said, it's still way better than most of the album. The intro briefly nods to 'Chic Cheer' in terms of vocals before Rodgers gives a brief spoken word Chic history lesson. This kind of works, enhancing the feeling of this freshened-up, old-style Chic. The trouble is that it isn't a great song in the first place; it's a solid effort, but it needed more dynamics and a better vocal arrangement. An instrumental version was also released.

It's About Time (Nile Rodgers & Chic) (2018)

Personnel:
Nile Rodgers: guitar, vocals
Folami, Kimberly Davis: vocals
Jerry Barnes: bass
Richard Hilton, Russell Graham: keyboards
Ralph Rolle: drums
Bill Holloman, Brandon Wright, Dan Moretti: saxophone
Curt Ramm, Steve Jankowski: trumpet
Recorded at Abbey Road Studios, London, between 2014 and 2018
Produced by Nile Rodgers and others
Release date: 28 September 2018
Label: Virgin/EMI
Highest chart places: UK: 10, US: did not chart
Running time: 38:58

The album emerged three years after the two single tracks, but it didn't match up to their great promise. There was *supposed* to be plenty of other unused pre-1983 Chic material incorporated, but if so, it is hard to discern. One song that didn't make the cut was 'Prince Said It'. Rodgers pulled the song, telling the *NME* in June 2017 that the song was 'about my conversations with Prince. But after he passed away, it felt wrong. It felt uncomfortable.'

One thing that remained true to form on the album was Rodgers' methods of recording the songs. Folami told *Trouve La Groove* in 2017 that 'you can go and record with him and never hear the song, and you'll never hear the song after you leave. You won't know how it goes 'cause of how he records it! So basically, he just gives you the lyric, and he just asks you to repeat that one line like 100 times and you just keep repeating. The work then gets switched over to the engineer – that's who puts the song together.' Holloman says: 'I always enjoyed recording with him (Rodgers) because he would always entertain my ideas and often we'd go with them.'

Yet, the album is hampered by three difficulties. The first is the decision to update and modernise the sound for contemporary listeners. The songs lack the warm grooves we associate with Chic and there is a fatiguing, hard quality to the sound. Secondly, there's the host of guest vocalists (noted under the relevant songs), which ultimately gives the album a lack of focus. Thirdly, the songs are mostly not good enough, with only two or three really doing the business and rising above average. Generally, this is an album where more proved to be less. A better album would have used 'I'll Be There' as a template. The standout on the album is Rodgers' guitar, which remains as infectious as ever.

Kenny Lehman gives his perspective on the album:

> Warner Bros. (who own Virgin/EMI) gave Nile an incredible amount of money and they wanted him to reinvent Chic. Nile said okay, but he

delivered a poor album. I heard the single ('I'll Be There') – it was slick, great and sounded just like Chic. But for the album, he jumped off into a whole new thing. Warner Bros. disliked what he did. He would play guitar on tracks like 'Get Lucky', but he wasn't the reason these songs sounded modern. They featured his guitar because they loved his style.

The front cover was, however, a success of sorts. It is a direct nod back to their debut, even down to the whistles! I would still have preferred to see Rodgers on the cover, though. This time around, the two models are Duckie Thot and Jazzelle Zanaughtti. It was shot by Britt Lloyd and directed by Greg Foley, co-founder of *V Magazine*.

The album was intended to be the first of two 'final' Chic albums. However, the second album, prospectively titled *Executive Realness* and intended for a 2019 release, has yet to appear. One track from it, 'I Believe In Music', was partly broadcast during a BBC documentary on Rodgers called *How To Make It In The Music Business*.

Holloman's observation on *It's About Time* – 'I didn't think it put us any further than where we were' – is the hard truth; the album just didn't have the anticipated impact, in spite of going top ten in Britain.

'Till The World Falls' (Rodgers/Brandon Anderson/Anaïs Aida/Neo Jessica Joshua/Alexander Crossan/Vic Mensa)

It's one of the best three tracks and a great choice to open the album. The guest vocalists on this track – Cosha, Mura Masa and Vic Mensa – don't really add anything special. Even so, this is a strong song with a big chorus, perhaps lacking anything distinctive in the backing track. Yet, these are musically simpler times for Chic, with little in the way of instrumental breakdowns and the tight groove of the rhythm tracks, which were highlights of their best work. Despite the simplicity, this still needed six writers! It was released as a single.

'Boogie All Night' (Rodgers/Daniel Eisner Harle)

Without messing around, the song jumps straight into the chorus. Neo Jessica Joshua guests under her singing alias 'Nao', but her 'little girl' voice is irritating. The song isn't much better; it's filler at best, with little substance and nothing to pull you back for more.

'Sober' (Rodgers/Charles Harrison/Lonnell Corbett)

Craig David and British rapper Stefflon Don are the guests for this one. It isn't bad and the chorus is an earworm hook, but it's still not hitting home as strongly as it should. Even without the guests, it would have been hard to work up to something more special. It's just not that interesting a song for me, even with the hook. Rodgers can do a lot better than 'not bad'. That being said, it was released as a single, so the record label thought it had something going for it. A different version, called 'New Jack Sober', was added to the end of the album.

'Do You Wanna Party' (Rodgers/Thomas Troelsen/Harle/Gamal Lewis)
Lunchmoney Lewis, another rapper, opens this, and while I can't say I am keen on his voice, it's not unpleasant. Musically, this is a decent, bright, positive tune riding on Rodgers' catchy rhythm playing. There's also the major surprise of a rock guitar solo from Rodgers at 2:30, which makes for an uplifting spell, and the outro showcases some wicked rhythm guitar.

'Dance With Me' (Rodgers/Curtis Williams/Sha Sha Jones)
The actress and singer Hailee Steinfeld is the singer. Her voice isn't strongly distinguishable and the song is similarly underwhelming. The backing track of Rodgers, Barnes, Rolle, etc., from 2:20 onwards is nice and funky, but that's the best of it.

'I Dance My Dance' (Rodgers/Alexandra Forbes/Jerry Barnes/Melissa Sanley)
Bass-man Jerry Barnes is a co-writer, and it's the only track with no guest vocalist, so we get Folami and Kimberly Davis on vocals. It makes for an instantly better and more cohesive sound. This is another of the best songs, with a musicality to it that is sadly missing on most of the album. An energetic chorus and a powerhouse rhythm track, with Barnes right up in the mix, sell the song.

'State Of Mine (It's About Time)' (Rodgers/Philippe Saisse)
This is a funk/jazz instrumental track featuring Chic alumni Philippe Saisse, who adds real genius and fire to the album with his wonderful piano parts. Rodgers responds in kind with some equally sublime guitar. The quality of the two playing off each other reminds me of Rodgers' earlier great musical interactions with Edwards or the keyboards of Sabino and Jones. Consequently, this is excellent. Saisse's solo (2:04) is a melodic, effervescent piece, which Rodgers responds to at 2:55 with a taut, jazzy solo that showcases a bluesy edge – marvellous work from both men.

'Queen' (Rodgers)
The only song Rodgers wrote alone for the album features Rodgers singing with Emeli Sande (whom he also appeared with on the Grenfell Fire charity record).

Elton John also appears, joining in with the other two. His high-harmony vocal is effective, as you would expect, but it doesn't feel right to have someone of his stature on backing and harmony vocals with Chic. He is a lead vocalist; it feels wasted having him if he isn't going to sing lead. It comes over as tokenism.

'I Want Your Love' (Edwards/Rodgers)
This collaboration with Lady Gaga was originally conceived for a Tom Ford fashion show and thus was never intended for this album. It loses the heartache and subtlety in the original arrangement, which she would have been perfectly capable of handling, evidenced by her own work. I would have liked to have heard her really let go in the verses, but she holds back. This is a good version, but a complete rearrangement from the bottom up – a full-on strings and brass arrangement with Lady Gaga really nailing the vocals and getting to the heart of the song's message – might well have produced something special.

Extra Chic

There have been many other albums that feature Chic personnel to varying degrees. The following are some of the more noteworthy selections, with plenty of gems to be discovered.

Send It (Ashford & Simpson) (Warner Bros., 1977)
Rodgers and Edwards arranged two tracks on the album. It was a big break for them, although they are not credited for their work on 'By Way Of Love's Express' and 'Don't Cost You Nothing'. Future Chic alumni Rob Sabino and Ulanda McCullough (credited as Yolanda) appear on the album.

Happy Together (Odyssey) (RCA, 1982)
Odyssey were the vocal trio of Billy McEachern, Lillian Lopez and Louise Lopez, probably best known for 'Native New Yorker' and 'Going Back To My Roots'. *Happy Together* was released on 1 May 1982 and features one Chic track – the late-period classic 'Together'. The song was written by Edwards and Rodgers and they also play on it, along with Rob Sabino. No Tony Thompson, alas, with a Linndrum machine used instead, but we do get Gene Orloff on board conducting and arranging the strings.

Even without Thompson, this remains one of the finest 1980s Chic performances. The song is a totally infectious groove, with Rodgers leading from the front. His grand-standing lead rhythm guitar is electric, while Edwards is at his sublime best with his supple melodic bass slipping and sliding around Rodgers. It captures something of the mood and feel of 'Why' from around the same period. Here, there is a sense of quiet, satisfied reflection, but the strings, by contrast, are a cinematic swell tugging at your heart. Lillian Lopez delivers the sultry lead vocals in what is, for the most part, a solo performance, and she is simply outstanding with her measured but emotional performance.

This amazing song is almost an epilogue to the glory years of Chic. I wonder if it was originally intended for the contemporary *Soup For One* soundtrack, where it would have fitted so well. The album version (6:19) is the one to indulge in, but it was also released as an edited single version. The album itself only charted in the UK but at a very reasonable number 21.

One Down (Material) (Elektra, 1982)
Rodgers and Thompson play on 'I'm The One' and 'Come Down', with Thompson also appearing on 'Don't Lose Control'. 'I'm The One' has an industrial feel to it, livened up by Rodgers' jazzy guitar licks. 'Come Down' is a more bass-and-drums-driven groove, again with Rodgers adding the sparkle. Ray Jones also appears, playing electric grand piano on 'Memories', written by Hugh Hopper for Soft Machine. The song benefits from the then-unknown Whitney Houston, who sings it superbly. The album is worth listening to as this was what, in part, persuaded David Bowie that Nile Rodgers was his ideal co-producer and collaborator for *Let's Dance*.

Original Sin (INXS) (WEA, 1983)
The lead-off single for *The Swing* album was produced by Rodgers. That would have been his only contribution, but the band were having trouble finding the song's groove, so Rodgers, guitar in hand, stepped in to play it along with them. That was the version that made the single and album, with an extra bonus, as keyboard player Andrew Farriss told Paul Cashmere for *Noise11* in November 2020:

> We had been doing backing vocals. Nile came in and said, 'This sounds pretty good, guys, but we need a little extra something.' He said, 'Do you mind if I call someone?' We said, 'Sure', and then Daryl Hall walks through the door and I'm like, 'What?!' That guy was huge back then, and he turned up really quick. The next thing, he is singing on 'Original Sin'. He is an amazing guy.

Rodgers has played it live with Chic in the last ten years or so, but it's a stretch to justify its inclusion. Rodgers is as pre-eminent as ever on the rhythm part, but the song itself is nothing special. The production doesn't help, being too strident, and, in spite of Rodgers, there is little groove in the rhythm section. It's a tiring listen, with the crashing drums pounding the life out of it.

Hearts And Bones (Paul Simon) (Warner Bros., 1983)
Edwards, Rodgers and Sabino turn up almost together again. 'Think Too Much (a)' features Rodgers and Edwards, while 'Cars Are Cars' features Rodgers and Sabino (who adds synths). 'Think Too Much (a)' opens with Rodgers, who no doubt was expressly asked to play his scratchy rhythm part. Edwards keeps it simple, with just a few flourishes, but it's a delight to hear him play with Rodgers on what is otherwise a very ordinary song. 'Cars Are Cars' is a more up-tempo slice of pop breeziness. Sabino doesn't get to stamp himself much on it, so the main Chic interest is Rodgers and his guitar, his playing complementing the sweet melody beautifully. Sabino additionally plays synths on 'Allergies' and adds piano to 'Rene And George Magritte With Their Dog After The War'.

The Leader (Fonzi Thornton) (RCA, 1983)
The album, said Thornton to *PopMatters* on 11 December 2020, 'was a culmination of ideas I'd been thinking about as an artist for a really long time.' Two tracks have a strong Chic presence. Edwards and Rodgers are in the rhythm section, along with Rob Sabino on both 'The Leader' and 'Perfect Lover'. The title track also features a plethora of Chic backing vocalists in Alfa Anderson, Dolette McDonald, Jocelyn Brown, Luther Vandross, Tawatha Agee and Michelle Cobbs. The song, as evidenced in the cheerleader-style intro, serves as a kind of introduction to Fonzi – his time in the spotlight. He sings

it well enough, but the song is good rather than great. Musically, the song could sit happily on later 1980s Chic albums.

'Perfect Lover' is much better, despite the irritating, albeit catchy, synth intro. Rodgers plays a memorable rhythm part while Edwards cooks nicely on the bass. Thornton is also effective, adding harmony parts to his soulful lead. This one is well worth checking out.

Do You (Sheena Easton) (EMI, 1985)

EMI wanted Rodgers to work a similar magic for Easton as he had for Madonna. Rodgers agreed to produce the album and also played guitar, keyboards and bass. He also contributed to the songwriting: 'Magic Of Love' was written by him alone, and he co-wrote 'Money Back Guarantee' with Martin Celay, who played guitar on *Take It Off* and *B-Movie Matinee* and also plays on this album. Three of the Bowie *Let's Dance* brass section also appear – Stan Harrison, Steve Elson and Mac Gollehon. The roster of backing vocalists also contains a large number of Chic alumni, most notably Norma Jean Wright, Fonzi Thornton and Michelle Cobbs, along with Curtis and Brenda King and Frank and George Simms.

The album didn't chart in the UK and neither did the single 'Do It For Love', but the album did reach number 40 in America, while the single got to number 29. That was reasonable, but a dismayed Easton reflected to *Classic Pop* magazine in April 2007: 'Looking back, it was a huge mistake. I think as artists, we (she and Rodgers) just didn't gel and it's the album I'm most disappointed by.' The album steered Easton away from her usual pop style towards a very Chic-style sound. She handles it well, and the album is at least listenable and occasionally excellent.

The opening pair of tracks is the best. 'Do It For Love' is a good song and would fit in easily on *Like A Virgin*. It has a sound similar to that of the classy pop feel of that album. 'Don't Break My Heart' is just wonderful, a 'must hear', utterly superb, catchy, hook-laden track with Rodgers' guitar well to the fore. He even gets a brief solo as a bonus, and the backing vocals are Chic at their best. Ironically, it's Rodgers' 'Magic Of Love' that is the first dip in quality. It's not especially memorable, in spite of the backing vocal choir being right up front. His 'Money Back Guarantee' is slightly better, an effervescent tune, but is lacking in anything memorable to pull you back to it.

The 2024 deluxe edition includes the uncut sessions as a bonus and most of the songs are extended. The fabulous 'Don't Break My Heart', for instance, is nearly a minute longer. These uncut versions are the ones to hear.

Boys And Girls (Bryan Ferry) (EMI, 1985)

Rodgers has appeared on several of Ferry's albums, but the most significant is this massive and superb UK number-one album. He appears on 'Sensation' and 'Don't Stop The Dance'. Omar Hakim can also be heard playing drums on 'Slave To Love', while the backing choir used throughout the album excitingly features Alfa Anderson, Michelle Cobbs and Fonzi Thornton. So, 'Sensation' has the double delight of Rodgers playing lead rhythm guitar and the Chic singers (plus one or two others) harmonising in the choruses. 'Sensation' is exactly what the title says – a beautifully produced and well-mixed experience, deluxe and expansive.

Rodgers is less evident on 'Don't Stop The Dance'. He is there in the mix but as part of the wall of sound that Ferry often favours, with little details popping out. The backing vocalists are here again, hitting the high notes, which round out Ferry's resonant baritone style. A great song.

She's The Boss (Mick Jagger) (CBS/Columbia, 1985)

Jagger's debut solo album was recorded in 1984 at Compass Point Studios, Nassau and Power Station, New York. Rodgers produced three of the songs (all at Power Station) and plays guitar. Several other Chic alumni also appear. Sammy Figueroa says he got the call from Jagger 'because he had heard me with Average White Band and he fell in love with that.'

Asked to sum up Rodgers' contributions, Jagger opined to *International Musician & Recording World* in June 1985 that 'He's a much more outgoing person (than Bill Laswell, the record's other producer) and a real New York kind of guy. Also, he's a guitar player, someone I could sit down and play things to. I found him stimulating in another way. He loves to play rock 'n' roll. He was telling me that when he was a teenager, he used to like Led Zeppelin, and he'd get the piss taken out of him by his black friends for liking this rock music. Nile was helpful with things like harmonies.'

The first of the four key tracks for Chic fans is 'Half A Loaf', which features Edwards, Rodgers, Sabino, Thornton and Eddie Martinez. Rodgers plays the jangly rhythm parts while Martinez handles the rock guitar licks and solo. Jagger uses a 'bellowing' mid-range vocal, which is at odds with the slick instrumentation, barring Martinez's strong rock guitar lead parts. The overall effect is harsh and noisy.

'Turn The Girl Loose', with its lightweight reggae tones, is much better. The bass player is Edwards, while Sabino is on the Prophet. The song is still rather limited in range and ambition, and Jagger's strident vocal is a hard listen. The big bonus is Alfa Anderson, who performs the indignant mid-song rap; unusual for her, but she gets it spot on. Another Chic regular, Lenny Pickett, plays baritone saxophone on the song.

'Hard Woman's Chic connection is solely Tony Thompson on drums. Jagger recalled for *International Musician* in June 1985: 'When I did it first, I had a much lighter approach, and then the vocals started to get harder and harder. I kinda like that because it doesn't make it too insipid.' The perfect addition to keep things harder was Thompson, but this is still a soft rock ballad at heart and a nondescript one at that, although Paul Buckmaster's string arrangement is excellent.

'Secrets' features Edwards, Rodgers and Sabino and is the best of the four. George Edward Smith (from Hall & Oates) handles the lead guitar, while his Saturday Night Live Band comrade Anton Fig is on drums. With the three Chic men, it makes for a potent band, and this is an electrifying blast of hybrid rock/funk with searing lead guitar from Smith.

Riptide (Robert Palmer) (Island, 1985)
Edwards produced the album and plays bass on eight tracks. Accompanying him from Chic are Tony Thompson, who drums on seven songs, and Fonzi Thornton, who sings backups on two. The album has its moments, but where it all comes together so gloriously right is on 'Addicted To Love'. Palmer vocally owns the song in a great arrangement by Chaka Khan. Equally, the chops on display in the accompaniment are stunning. Edwards plays the walking bass melody/riff while Thompson crashes out a ferocious snapping drum part. Thompson recalled to *Modern Drummer* in 2002 how they got his drum sound at Compass Point Studios: 'The engineer, Jason Casaro, took a tube the size of my bass drum and built this tunnel from my bass drum all the way out into the hall and up the stairs. It was this weird thing he hooked up. And it worked. The groove in the house was so thick, and what am I playing? A simple boom-bop-tish-bop-boom-bop! It was unbelievable; I locked into that with everyone else swinging, and it brought the walls down. That song was a masterpiece.' Add in Thornton on backups and this is an exceptional, high-quality Chic alumni track. The lead guitarist is Andy Taylor (Duran Duran), so the song is effectively recorded by the second Power Station lineup with Edwards. 'Addicted To Love' is one minute longer on the album than on the single. That's one minute more of magic you need to listen to!

When The Boys Meet The Girls (Sister Sledge) (Atlantic, 1985)
The album got to number 19 in the UK and was produced by Rodgers. The album features him on guitar, bass and synth, along with Ray Jones, Rob Sabino, Jimmy Bralower and the horns Rodgers often used in this era. The big track is 'Frankie', written by songwriter Denise Eisenberg (aka Joy Denny) about Frank Sinatra, which got them a number-one hit single in the UK.

Musically, we are firmly in the 1980s synth sound Rodgers perfected with Madonna. There are several very good songs, however. The title track is a bubbly piece with an earworm chorus, topped off with Rodgers' rhythm guitar and an especially fine solo from him, where he plays around the melody. Sabino's synths are warmly exciting, too. This is the best song on the album by far.

'Frankie', which doesn't feature Rodgers or any Chic alumni, is impossible to get out of your head. It's a catchy pop song that shows off Kathy Sledge's lead vocal and the Sledge harmonies. 'The Boy Most Likely' is of most interest because Rodgers wrote the song. There's drama in the verse instrumentation, which contrasts well with the lighter chorus and that trademark ringing guitar from Rodgers. Sadly, it's not a great song. 'You Need Me' is above average, with the 1980s-era Rodgers horn section in fine form. Other than these songs, the album lacks quality material.

Home Of The Brave (Laurie Anderson) (Warner Bros., 1986)
Rodgers produced this album and plays on two tracks. Rob Sabino joins him on the album opener 'Smoke Rings', playing all the synth parts on what is a largely electronic track. Anderson effectively 'speaks' the lyrics on this intriguing song, albeit there is nothing 'Chic-like' about it. Rodgers' guitar is present but buried so deep that it's easy to miss. The second track, 'Language Is A Virus', sees Rodgers joined by Brenda White-King, Curtis King, Frank Simms and Tawatha Agee on backing vocals. Rodgers plays Synclavier and keyboards and is effectively the only musician on it. As such, it's no surprise that he gets some groove going in the rhythm.

Notorious (Duran Duran) (EMI, 1986)
Rodgers' remix of 'The Reflex' was good, but better news for Chic fans was his work on the band's fourth album. While Chic alumni Mac Gollehon (horns), Curtis King Jr. and Brenda White-King (backing vocals) are present, this is all about Rodgers' production and guitar for Chic fans. He plays on most of the album. Rodgers is shown off to best effect on the two tracks where he is the only guitarist. 'So Misled' isn't a great song, but Rodgers' rhythm lines give it some sparkle. That leaves the title track, which Rodgers has covered live with Chic in recent years. It's a catchy song, which was released as a single, reaching number seven in the UK and the dizzy heights of number two in America. Rodgers isn't credited as a writer, but the germ of the melody came from him. Simon Le Bon recalled to Clark Collis for *Entertainment* (March 2011): 'I remember him (Rodgers) playing some notes up the neck of his guitar and it was the riff from 'Notorious'. We just said, 'Man, we've got to have that."

The Chic sound extends on from Rodgers' guitar to John Taylor's bassline, which is akin to something Edwards might have played. The chorus makes maximum use of Rodgers's earworm riff, which is the pulse of the song.

L Is For Lover (Al Jarreau) (Warner Bros., 1986)
Rodgers produced this album, along with the contemporary TV theme single 'Moonlighting'. He also plays guitar, bass and keyboards, and he even performs the vocoder part on 'Real Tight'. Also featured on the album are Philippe Saisse (keyboards, piano) and, on backing vocals, Tawatha Agee, Fonzi Thornton, Michelle Cobbs, Curtis King and Brenda King. The album is rather too laid back, and the songs lack the quality to pull you back. The exception might be the closer 'Real Tight', which has some punch and groove to it. It's too little, too late for the album, though.

Out Loud (Outloud) (Warner Bros., 1987)
This was a three-way project between Rodgers, Philippe Saisse and Felicia Collins. All three members of the band mostly handle the instrumentation, and they share the vocals. Guest musicians are Steve Elson (tenor saxophone), Robert Aaron (alto saxophone) and Larry Etkin (trumpet). Kevin Jones also helped out by programming the drum tracks.

The primary interest here is the guitar parts from Rodgers and Collins. Collins told *Guitarhoo!* in 2004: 'The record started off funky. The first couple of cuts we did were bangin'. I'll never forget the day I came to the studio and they played this turgid demo ('It's Love This Time') for me. I was informed that a Warner Bros. bigwig wanted us to record the drivel. With that as the lead-off single, no wonder it was extradited and locked up!'

The 'turgid' song was written by Madonna collaborator Patrick Leonard and Gardner Cole. The lion's share of the rest is written by Rodgers, sometimes with Saisse and Collins, plus one with Sylvester Stewart. With this in mind, it's no surprise that the album is in the vein of Rodgers' solo albums, heavy on synths and programmed drums. Sadly, it's underwhelming, with little that is memorable.

The standout songs include 'Feeling Good', which has a Chic-like groove and would have been even better with real musicians in place of the programmed tracks. 'Camouflage' benefits from Collins' lead vocals. Her voice is the best of the three, and she gives the song a boost. 'Good Together' is genuinely excellent. It's a strong duet between Collins and Rodgers over a sweetly powerful melody. The twin lead guitar duel is fabulous, too. This is a must-hear song.

Jody Watley (Jody Watley) (MCA, 1987)
The Shalamar vocalist's debut solo album features three songs produced by Edwards, which can be found on what Watley called 'vibe two' of the album. Performing on the three – 'Love Injection', 'Don't You Want Me' and 'Learn To Say No' (a duet with George Michael) – are Edwards, Rodgers and Thornton. Eddie Martinez also handles the lead guitar parts.

'Love Injection' has a catchy bass pulse rhythm and great licks from Martinez, but the synths, courtesy of Jeff Bova, are low-budget film theme stuff. 'Don't You Want Me' is kind of in the Madonna style and suffers from fatiguing mid-1980s drums and big synth chords. 'Learn To Say No' is the best of the three songs. Edwards catches fire on this one, inspired at last, as is Eddie Martinez, who even cops some licks from Rodgers. Watley and George Michael combine well, and they give the song its boundless energy. The uncredited sax solo, incidentally, is by Larry Schneider.

Move To This (Cathy Dennis) (Polydor, 1990)
Polydor spared no expense on Dennis's debut album, choosing the best producers. The album did well in the UK, reaching number three, while it got

to number 67 in America. Rodgers produced two tracks – 'Everybody Move' and 'My Beating Heart' – both of which he added guitar to.

Joining Rodgers on 'Everybody Move' is Edwards on bass, Richard Hilton on keyboards/drum programming, plus Fonzi Thornton, Michelle Cobbs and Curtis King on backing vocals. Edwards' deep bass groove is his best. Credit must also go to Hilton for his intelligent use of strings, which work effectively. The weakest part of this song is actually Cathy Dennis, whose voice is too weak for the music. A stronger, more commanding voice was needed for this one.

Only Hilton joins Rodgers for the reflective ballad 'My Beating Heart'. Hilton's synths and keyboards are always interesting, and he creates a backdrop that gives Dennis the room to deliver a thoughtful vocal. Rodgers is too low in the mix but pops up with harmony parts to good effect.

Hero/Community (State Of Art) (Polygram, 1990)

The partnership of Norma Jean Wright and Ray Jones produced the 'Hero' single, followed by the album *Community* in 1991. All of the songs are at least listenable. Two are particularly impressive. Luci Martin guests on 'Understanding', and consequently, there's a definite extra sparkle to the song, while the torch ballad 'Laughing At The Years' is excellent.

Black Tie White Noise (David Bowie) (Savage/Arista, 1992)

Following his marriage to Iman on 24 April 1992, Bowie set to work on this album, on which several songs are influenced by that happy event. He decided to work again with Rodgers, but this time, Bowie brought in more of his own collaborators, including the likes of Mick Ronson and Mike Garson, whom he hadn't worked with for many years. Rodgers brought in the Chic alumni, including Richard Hilton and Philippe Saisse (keyboards), Sterling Campbell (drums), Gerardo Velex (percussion), plus several of the vocal choir – Fonzi Thornton, Tawatha Agee, Curtis King Jr., Dennis Collins and Brenda White-King.

Bowie saw the project differently from *Let's Dance,* as he described in the *Black Tie White Noise* film in 1993: 'This time around, it was more my vision of what my album was gonna sound like, and Nile provided the buoyancy and the enthusiasm for the project.' There are some tracks that stand out, largely down to Rodgers' guitar. 'You've Been Around' has his guitar as the pulse, and he gets to play some lush, jazzy licks on the ballad 'Don't Let Me Down And Down'. Better still is the cover version of Cream's 'I Feel Free'. It's rearranged with funky bass work and the ever-present jangling guitar of Rodgers. Rodgers co-wrote the instrumental 'Looking For Lester' – Lester being trumpeter Lester Bowie. But frustratingly, Rodgers is subdued in the mix, and the song's big 'draw' is the duelling trumpet of Lester against David Bowie's saxophone. The backing choir only feature on the cover version of Morrissey's 'I Know It's Gonna Happen Someday'. They give it a gospel feel behind Bowie's exhortations and Wil T. Springer's lead guitar.

Beverly Hills Cop III Soundtrack (Nile Rodgers & Richard Hilton) (MCA, 1994)

Rodgers scored this film, having already written and arranged incidental music for *Coming To America* (1988) and *Blue Chips* (1994). He does a good job on each, but for this film, he contributes a version of Harold Faltermeyer's classic 'Axel-F' from the first *Beverly Hills Cop* movie. He recorded it with his synth partner in Chic, Richard Hilton, and they came up with an updated, breakbeats-driven, pulsating version. It's okay, but it's not a patch on the original.

Living In Fear (Power Station) (Capitol, 1996)

The first Power Station album featured Tony Thompson on drums, along with several Chic backing vocalists. This time around, John Taylor (from Duran Duran) had to leave the sessions, so producer Bernard Edwards played all the bass parts. Other Chic alumni on the album are Jose Rossy (of 'I Want Your Love' fame on percussion), Phillipe Saisse (keyboards), Lenny Pickett, Alex Foster and Mark Gollehon (all on horns). The band for the album is completed by Robert Palmer on vocals and Andy Taylor (Duran Duran) on guitar.

Power Station are intriguing as they come over as a heavy pop band. But with Edwards on bass, locking in with Thompson, it gives them some serious funky rhythms underpinning Palmer's mostly bellicose vocals and Taylor's angular, slashing guitar. Several songs are worth investigating. Opener 'Notoriety' is a good example of their style, with Edwards' wandering bass runs giving the song movement and interest. 'She Can Rock It' is from the same zone as 'Addicted To Love' and is every bit as good. 'Power Trippin'' grooves along on Edwards' bass, as does the bubbly 'Life Forces'. Edwards gets to swing on the funky ballad 'Love Conquers All', which features some cool brass offsetting the blustery lead guitar. Album closer 'Taxman' features sitar in the intro but settles down into a rather leaden arrangement, which Edwards does his best to keep lively.

Let's Bounce/I Want Your Love (GTS featuring Norma Jean Wright & Luci Martin) (Armitage, 1997)

This was a limited single release in Japan and features the Chic duo on a song they co-wrote, plus the Chic classic. 'Let's Bounce' lives up to its title and is a lively piece of work. However, the best thing about it is definitely the vocals. The rhythm track is pedestrian and uninteresting, leaving the song sounding stodgy. Sadly, the same is true of 'I Want Your Love', which is musically a shadow of the original song, with the girls caught in the middle of a musical stew. It's great to hear them sing, of course, but that's about it.

You're The Best (The Larry Joseph Project featuring Luci Martin) (Liquid Time Records, 1991)

This song appears on the *Young Giants Of Platinum Funk Vol. 1* EP. The best thing about it is Martin, who is always worth listening to. It's a shame about the song, though, which is rather dull and lacking in interest.

Sensitivity (Shapeshifters & Chic) (Positiva, 2006)

This single got to number 40 in the UK chart. The song makes use of the melody from the then-still unreleased Mathis/Chic collaboration 'Love And Be Loved', which explains why both Rodgers and Edwards are credited with the songwriting. Richard Hilton is credited with recording Rodgers' guitar parts at his Le Crib studios.

There is a 3:41 radio edit that got airplay, and also worth checking out is the 6:25 extended album mix. This song works well on three levels: vocalist Kelly-Marie Smith handles it with great confidence and aplomb, and then there's the epic string arrangement from Colin Smith, who even gets in a reference to the string arrangement of 'I Want Your Love' on the radio edit at 3:31 and on the extended version at 5:01. The third big plus is Rodgers' fluid but rhythmic guitar lines. His ability to transform the song and give it heart and soul is just amazing. The song itself is excellent and one of Rodgers' best collaborations.

Shapeshifters also worked with Chic vocalist Kimberly Davis for their singles 'Life Is A Dancefloor' (2019) and 'Second Chance' (2020).

Get Lucky, Lose Yourself To Dance & Give Life Back To Music (Daft Punk) (Columbia, 2013/14)

The 2014 Grammy Award for Record Of The Year went to 'Get Lucky'. Rodgers explained to *Guitar World*'s Amit Sharma in October 2020: 'When I finally did the Daft Punk record, they were like, 'Dude, can you bring that see-through Strat!' So, it doubled The Hitmaker on 'Get Lucky'. There are three guitar tracks, two of which were The Hitmaker and one of which was the plexiglass.' He added to Paul Lester for *The Guardian* in 2014 that the session was 'like love at first sight. Just like Bowie, they let me do what I do. They loved it. 'Go ahead, Nile, do your thing, man.' When we found that groove, I felt like Indiana Jones – like, 'Wow, I just discovered the Ark of the Covenant!'

And what an incredible groove it is, still as potent ten years later and set to be a radio staple for many more to come. Rodgers is the melodic motor at the heart of it, his guitar lines weaving in and around that infectious rhythm. The combination of him and vocalist Pharrell Williams is a match made in heaven. Kudos, too, to Chic drummer Omar Hakim, who gives the song energy and swing. It's a tremendous song and one of the best projects Rodgers has ever been involved with. The single was a worldwide smash hit, reaching number one in many territories, including Britain, and number two in America, which shows just how massively well-received it was.

'Get Lucky' was featured on Daft Punk's album *Random Access Memories,* which topped the charts in Britain and America. Not surprisingly, the album's other collaboration with Rodgers and Williams was released as the follow-up single to 'Get Lucky'. 'Lose Yourself To Dance' is more of a slow burner, a little weighed down by the stodgy drum track. Rodgers' infectious guitar groove is irresistible, though, and Williams again shows what a talented vocalist he is. It only reached the lower reaches of singles charts around the world.

The third song with Rodgers was 'Give Life Back To Music', which opened the album. It, too, was released as a single, and also unsuccessfully. The vocoder vocals don't do it justice. It needed a strong vocal line to match what is a decent tune, with Rodgers' trademark guitar as the centrepiece of the sound.

Do What You Wanna Do (Nile Rodgers) (CR2 Records, 2014)
Rodgers recorded this song in 2013 in Ibiza at the International Music Summit. He auctioned the song off to raise money for his We Are Family Foundation, and CR2 Records were the highest bidders. Label head Mark Brown told *Rolling Stone* in July 2014: 'Initially, when we signed the record, there weren't any verses in the track – it was just kind of Nile's hook – so we worked with him to develop some extra verses and make it into a complete song.'

'Time to play a little disco', intones Rodgers at the beginning and that's exactly what we get. The melody is the kind of happy, warm hook you would associate with a beach holiday. Despite Mark Brown's suggestion that there was extra work done, this is minimal and there is little more to it than the hook and the effervescent chorus. It's listenable, but Rodgers could do a lot better.

Good Times & Get On Up (Aristofreeks & Next Step) (Pacific Electronic Music, 2015)
Next Step was the project by Anderson, Martin and Wright – three former Chic vocalists back together again. Two songs were released, produced by the remix duo Aristofreeks, who had put out a Rodgers-approved mix of the original 'Le Freak'.

Musically, 'Good Times' is jarring, but the trio are as wonderful as ever, sharing the verses and choruses together. For 'Get On Up', they are joined by Kathy Sledge, and again, the vocalists are the best thing about it. There is a good song hidden in the overloaded mix, fighting to get out! The trio also recorded as Reunion, and you can hear the excellent 'My Lover's Arms' (2010) on *YouTube*. It's a strong tune and shows off their sublime talents.

Aristofreeks also put out the following songs – all are new versions or new songs – with Kathy Sledge alone on vocals: 'Thank You', 'We Are Family', 'Keep It Movin'' and 'Thinking Of You'.

Music From My Heart (Alfa Anderson) (Self-Released, 2017)
Karen Milne guests on this album. Alfa told Christian Wikane for *Popmatters* in December 2018: 'When I wrote 'Sending Love', I knew it needed a violin, and I knew Karen was just the person to ask. She played such a hauntingly

beautiful melody on the song.' Also featured, on backup vocals, is Norma Jean Wright. It's a beautiful song, with Milne's violin echoing the heartache in the vocals.

Wright also adds her silky vocals to 'Perfectly Chic' and 'When Luther Sings'. The former is a strong homage, which hits the right spots musically and has some lovely tributes in the lyrics, too. She is also on 'When Luther Sings', which is a fine tribute to Vandross and equally has a lot of the Chic style in the arrangement and performance. The other tracks are all worth listening to, especially the stellar ballad 'A Better Love', but it's the aforementioned three that most strongly and successfully capture Anderson's heritage.

See also Anderson's wonderful 2013 single 'Former Lady Of Chic', which evokes strong memories of classic Chic in the string arrangement. The song summarises her situation, looking back on the glory years but pointing out she is still very much here and as great as she ever was. Since then, she has recorded lead vocals for the Tinkr album *Blended* (2018), which is also worth listening to.

Four To The Floor (Folami) (Regal Music Group, 2017)
Rodgers plays guitar on this effervescent song by his former vocalist in Nile Rodgers & Chic. It's actually better than much of the material on *It's About Time;* it's simpler and less produced. That being said, it's still not a classic by any means, and it doesn't showcase Folami at her best, either. Rodgers is as effective as ever, but there's nothing especially brilliant about his playing.

This World (Sylvano featuring Norma Jean Wright & Luci Martin) (Self-Released, 2017)
Swiss musician Sylvano put out a four-track EP and somehow got the services of the Chic duo for the lead track. It's a funky groove with catchy synth melody lines, a real grower of a track that deserves to be better known. Getting Wright and Martin to sing on it was an inspiration, and they are just devastating. Hearing them working with such great material is a real treasure.

Roses (Adam Lambert featuring Nile Rodgers) (Empire, 2020)
The Queen lead singer teamed up with Rodgers for this thoughtful record. A great vocal from the underrated Lambert (who deserves big solo success) and a typical Rodgers rhythm groove. The two are a perfect match.

Cuff It (Beyonce featuring Nile Rodgers) (Columbia, 2022)
Rodgers co-wrote this Grammy r&b category award winner. His guitar is an integral (albeit too low) part of the rhythm track on what is a bright and breezy tune, heavy on the brass. Rodgers has included this in Chic's setlists in recent times.

The Legacy

Looking back at the glory years of the Chic albums and their outside productions, Rodgers, in the *Very Best Of Chic* notes in 2000, was proud that 'we wrote the songs from our hearts and souls.' The joy and passion in the best of their music will hopefully live on as future generations discover their catalogue. After the pandemic and lockdowns of 2019/2020, there was a terrific moment on television in the UK. It was the broadcast of the new cover of 'Everybody Dance' by Cedric Gervais and Franklin featuring Nile Rodgers. The exuberant, exultant nature of the song was such a sensory overload after that difficult period in time. Things were still tricky, but that song and performance said that things were getting better. Chic have always been able to uplift your spirits.

Nile Rodgers continues to guest appear with other artists and play live with Chic. They remain a must-see act, guaranteed to get any crowd going.